LEGACY
of the
WHITE EAGLE

Legacy of the White Eagle

Julian E. Kulski

Published by

HMP. Inc.
Middleburg, Virginia

In association with
National History Day
www.nhd.org

Legacy of the White Eagle

Published by
HMP. Inc.

In association with
National History Day

All Rights Reserved

Copyright © 2006 by Julian E. Kulski

Book designed by Edward Małek

ISBN 1-4243-0525-X

Library of Congress Cataloging-in-Publication Data
Kulski, Julian E.
Legacy of the White Eagle

Published in the United States of America

www.whiteeaglelegacy.com

10 9 8 7 6 5 4 3 2 1

It is my fervent wish that all spirited young people will gain strength and inspiration by understanding the courage and bravery of all those before them who have fought for freedom and independence.

FOREWORD

Legacy of the White Eagle is a story of the coming of age of a young man during some of the most turbulent and trying years in Polish and world history. Julian Kulski's story also deepens our understanding of important historical events from World War II that have received little to no attention in high school textbooks. An account of the Warsaw Uprising, *Legacy of the White Eagle* is also about growing up during a time of great upheaval, a time when circumstances required young people to become adults and find the maturity to take on responsibilities beyond those of an average high school student. But it is also much more than one person's struggle to live through difficult times. Julian's story inspires and teaches us about courage, determination, personal strength and the meaning of freedom. And it reminds us why the study of history is so important.

The hero of *Legacy of the White Eagle* is a role model who shows us that ordinary people can do extraordinary things. Indeed, the past is about real people facing very real conflicts and by studying history, we learn about people whose strength and determination teach us about leadership and commitment. By uncovering the past, we see how average people can overcome tragedy through personal triumph, and how injustice inspires others to risk their own lives to improve the lives of many. And we are motivated to do as those who came before us - to become involved, to participate, to take a stand for what we believe in and to take action to improve our communities, our country and even the world. Julian's story is just one example of many in history of how a single individual can make a difference.

History is often taught from the perspective of the "history makers:" the presidents, prime ministers and other well-known individuals whose decisions and actions had dramatic influence on the course of events. Historians understand that millions of ordinary people played a role as well, but often they are lumped into groups called slaves, holocaust victims, freedom fighters, or suffragettes, which removes the personal details that help connect us to the past. Julian's story makes the past personal and gives voice to those who otherwise might remain nameless, and in doing so, his story brings the past alive.

Julian takes us on a personal journey that examines the conflicts he faced nearly every day and reveals emotions that take us from the personal to the profound. Julian's story is about the pursuit of freedom through self-determination, a theme found throughout world history and familiar to us as Americans, for our own past is defined by individuals who struggled for freedom, democracy and equality, from the time of the American Revolution right up to yesterday's headlines.

I hope Julian's story will inspire you to uncover the ordinary people in your own communities who have done the extraordinary. You can be your own historical detective, sifting through clues, sleuthing out sources, interviewing eyewitnesses, and drawing conclusions about the past. Your towns and cities are filled with people who played a part in history--who fought for their country, protested war, agitated for civil rights, defended the poor and otherwise took part in our struggles for freedom. Find them and help them tell their stories. You can give them a voice.

Cathy Gorn
Executive Director
National History Day

Contents

LEGACY OF THE WHITE EAGLE

Julian E. Kulski

Preface

As a child I loved Hollywood movies: the Wild West fights between cowboys and Indians, the high-speed car chases of cops and robbers through the canyons of Chicago skyscrapers, the jazz, and all the glitter. In Warsaw, the capital of Poland, we didn't have such high buildings, so many cars, so much luxury, or so many rich people. To a child, America was far away, another planet. During World War II, I was so absorbed by street fighting against the Germans — and by the emotions and worries of being a teenager — that I was only dimly aware of the military efforts of the United States against Germany and Japan. The first time I saw America's might was when more than a hundred Superfortress bombers flew twinkling and glittering in the midday sun over our burning city in a valiant effort to help us. I shall never forget the joy and relief of that moment.

At the end of the war, an opportunity came along that changed my entire life: a one-way ticket to America. I arrived in Boston with five dollars in my pocket and soon found out that life in America was not as easy as in its movies. For years, I had to work hard, hard, hard: as a short-order cook at Howard Johnson's, as a hotel waiter, as a roofer laying hot pitch. I faced the hardships that millions of immigrants have faced upon landing on these shores. It wasn't the Polish upper-class life I was born into, and I had to develop a work ethic that has served me well for the rest of my life.

I love America and am proud to be a citizen of the United States. I love American democracy, which gives opportunities to anyone willing to work his head off. I love the freedom in every aspect of American life: from the choice of a job to where and how to live, how to worship, and how to play. As an architect, I prefer drawing beautiful buildings to writing. Yet I owe so much to America that I felt I had to write this book. I hope my story of teenagers fighting for Polish independence will help young people today appreciate both the United States, "the home of the free and the land of the brave," and my native Poland, now proud and free again at last.

Father - 1919.

Mother - 1919.

Part I

Poland Before the War

Life on Felinski Street

When I turned ten on March 3, 1939, the world was a happy place — or so it seemed to me. My family had moved into a large home on Felinski Street in a beautiful new neighborhood of Warsaw. Our neighborhood, called Zoliborz, was a fashionable place to live, with tree-lined streets, parks, and gardens. Our house was only about a mile from the Vistula River, which flowed past the historic parts of town — the Old City with its narrow streets, squares with statues of Polish heroes, and such famous buildings as the royal palaces and City Hall. I liked to go across the river from the Old City to the Praga neighborhood to visit our large Warsaw Zoo. The zoo's director was a friend of my father. In the zoo, I had my own llama that I enjoyed riding. When the lioness had cubs, the curators would take her away for a while and let me play with the little ones.

In that house on Felinski Street lived my father and mother and I and my little sister, Wanda, and my Aunt Stacha, my Aunt Wanda, a German nanny and our family dachshund, Skut, as well as some servants. Behind the big house, we had a small swimming pool and a lovely garden with a hothouse. In the hothouse stood an award-winning statue by a famous sculptor. It was a statue of my sister at four years old. I kept homing pigeons in the attic and on the flat roof. They would fly in formation over the whole neighborhood of Zoliborz and return to their home base — until they started ruining Father's garden and I had to give them up.

All of us had plenty of space. We didn't even need the extra rooms in the basement, and I was allowed to play down there. I had a collection of little toy soldiers and enjoyed staging wars between them. I even had a whole unit of self-propelled tanks and fast-firing field guns. I put the armies through maneuvers and arranged ambushes. I had my soldiers "leapfrog"— not the children's game of hopping over each other's backs but approaching a target in military fashion, by turns keeping one group in action while another moved past it to a forward position. My fragile soldiers, made of lead, broke easily in the thick of battle, so I learned to melt them down and then to mold them into new soldiers and paint them in fresh, bright uniforms. Someday, I was sure, I would wear a uniform and fight for Poland the way my father and Uncle Norbert and other relatives had done, but it never occurred to me that it could happen before I was much older.

I always had pets, and one of my basement projects was raising royal white domestic rabbits. They stamp their feet when they are hungry, and like all rabbits they multiply rapidly. Soon I could not keep up with feeding them all, even with the help of servants, and the rabbits' stamping could be heard all over the house!

My mother was amazingly patient with this project but eventually put a stop to the noise and messiness of so many rabbits.

Mother, whose ancestors included the Polish King Stanislaw Leszczynski, was a fun-loving woman who adored dancing and parties. She was also beautiful and well aware of that. It was Mother who taught Wanda and me to ride horses, ski, and dance. She especially enjoyed Viennese waltzes, the music popular in her native city, Lwow, in the southern part of Poland most influenced by Austrian culture. Father didn't like to dance but became jealous when she danced with others. Although she was quite intelligent, Mother hadn't gone to university. Sometimes she drove Father crazy with her emotional reactions to situations. She spoke quickly and exaggerated details for dramatic effect, while he always thought first before speaking and had a more intellectual and analytical approach to problems. She was lighthearted and liked people and helping them. Everyone loved her for that. Father was the quiet and scholarly one and widely respected.

People sometimes said that I was more like Mother, and Wanda was more like Father because she tended to be a quiet child and an avid reader, while I was always on the go and into mischief. Wanda, three and a half years younger than I, was very pretty, with blue eyes and long, curly blonde hair. We often called her *Lalka* (doll). Wanda admitted to me much later that she had thought I was Mother's favorite. That was why she made up stories to get me into trouble so Mother would prefer her instead.

Mother tried hard to keep me out of mischief, but she was not a very effective disciplinarian and I often rebelled. I didn't want her to treat me like a child, and I wished I could grow up faster.

Our German nanny was much more restrictive, sometimes downright cruel. I fought her rules all the time and grew to hate her. My parents caught her being mean to me one day, and they fired her on the spot. My experience with that nanny prepared me to dislike Germans even before they attacked our country.

I loved Aunt Stacha, my father's sister, because she was kind and interesting to talk to and never tried to discipline me. She was married to Norbert Barlicki, a national leader who was my godfather and one of my father's favorite people. Unfortunately, Uncle Norbert was not a faithful husband, and Aunt Stacha had left him to live with us. Whenever Uncle Norbert came by to chat, Aunt Stacha would race to her room to avoid talking to him.

The only authority in our house that I truly respected and obeyed was my father. Everybody in Warsaw seemed to know that my father was a hero of our recent war of independence. Father had become one of the most important people in the city and was now the Deputy Lord Mayor of Warsaw and also the head of our antiaircraft and civil defense forces.

One day, when I was about eight years old, I tried to take advantage of Father's importance and quickly discovered the limit of his patience. My school friends and I liked to sneak aboard streetcars without paying, just to see if we could get away with it. That day, I got caught. When the streetcar conductor bawled me out and demanded payment, I told him brashly that I didn't need to pay because my father owned the streetcars. The angry conductor grabbed my school cap as I escaped. He didn't let the matter drop. He came to our house, told Father the whole story and presented the school cap with my name in it as evidence.

Father was so furious that I had pulled rank on the conductor that he chased me all over the house. Poor Wanda stood in a corner and shrieked in terror that he would kill me! Of course he didn't hurt me, but he gave me a good scare and taught me that being his son meant respecting others, not claiming special privileges. I adored Father and wanted to be just like him. But I often wished he was not so busy and could spend more time talking to me.

Poland's White Eagles

That period of independence between the two World Wars was a time of hope and energy for the Polish people. In school, our teachers took every opportunity to tell us about our country's past. For well over a century, most of Poland, including Warsaw, had belonged to Russia, and the tsar had required the teaching of history from a Russian point of view. Now, the Polish flag with its white eagle flew over our city again, and our teachers loved telling us about our own heritage and heroes.

Over many centuries, our nation in the heart of Europe was envied and brutally attacked by the Mongol hordes of Genghis Khan, by the armies of Islam, by the German Order of the Knights of the Black Cross, and by the Russian and Swedish empires. We had so many enemies! But the Polish people always fought against tyranny and survived.

Our teachers also told us about our period of constitutional monarchy from 1493-1569. Yes, they assured us, we Poles had a parliament and our king had to obey its laws back when most of Europe still had autocratic monarchs. And then, in 1569, we formed a union between the Kingdom of Poland and the Grand Duchy of Lithuania. Until 1795, our country was a huge, multinational commonwealth stretching from the Baltic Sea to the Black Sea and from Berlin almost to Moscow. This great prosperous country, with its rich agricultural land and valuable trade routes, was a safe haven for multitudes of religious faiths escaping persecution. It was this tolerance and love of liberty that distinguished our land from the rest of Europe.

During the reign of Russia's Empress Catherine the Great in the late 1700s, our King Stanislaw II August Poniatowski realized he was ill equipped to fight the military might of the rapidly expanding Russian and Prussian empires. Instead, this last King of Poland marshaled his resources to instill in the Polish people respect, loyalty, and love for their heritage. He believed that the realm of ideas, rather than military power, would sustain Poland's love of its culture and its determination to be free. So it's not surprising that some Polish leaders of that time went to America to join George Washington in his fight for independence, the most famous being General Tadeusz Kosciuszko and General Casimir Pulaski. Kosciuszko became a good friend of Thomas Jefferson and is known as the Father of American Artillery. Pulaski, who died near Savannah, Georgia, in the Revolutionary War, is often called the Father of American Cavalry.

This legacy of national pride and identity has passed from generation to generation and has enabled Poland to survive years of bloodshed and enslavement, never fully accepting foreign domination and never giving up hope for eventual resurrection.

My generation was born in an independent Warsaw thanks to men like my father, true white eagles who sacrificed their youth — and in many cases their lives — to free Poland from foreign tyranny. Marshal Jozef Pilsudski, the George Washington of modern-day Poland, formed the Polish Legions, and my father was one of the first to join and fight during and just after World War I. The Legions' heroic efforts were rewarded by the grateful nation, and the men who had freed the country were now running it with pride and zeal. New neighborhoods like our Zoliborz rose out of that determination to beautify and rebuild our city and our country.

My Inheritance

The blood that my father spilled when wounded on the battlefield helped assure my birth as a free Pole — and a fortunate one, with the proverbial silver spoon in my mouth. As a little boy, I wanted to fight heroically as my father had when he was a boy. I wanted to go to a military school and prayed that I would not be deprived of war.

Although Uncle Norbert and others told me stories about my father's exploits as a soldier, I could never get Father to tell me about his experiences himself. He was a modest man who would never brag or exaggerate, and his focus was on the present and future, not the past. Many years after I had grown up, my father wrote his memoirs. The following section about his time as a Polish Legionnaire confirms the inspiring stories of his bravery that I heard as a boy and reveals much about his character:

> The morning mists lifted, and the hurricane of enemy machine gunfire caused great damage to our ranks. Many of my soldiers had been hit and were calling for help. Through a hail of bullets we still advanced towards the enemy's positions, and I ran along the line looking for medics for my men. To my surprise, I couldn't find any, and I felt furious.
>
> Then I noticed my company commander lying seriously wounded. I knelt by him and was telling him the number of casualties in our company when I was machine-gunned through my stomach and fell to my side. I had forgotten to lie low while I reported. The company commander's orderly crawled over and dug a little trench around me to prevent further hits from unceasing machine gunfire. Shortly thereafter, I fainted.
>
> When I woke up, it was late at night and the sky was full of stars. As I lay on my back in that shallow ditch, I noticed two things: extreme cold, and silence so complete as to be eerie. The battle had stopped. I couldn't move, and I felt helpless before I fell back into unconsciousness.
>
> It was 5 October, 1915, during the massive Ukrainian campaign against the Russian armies. When I became conscious again, it was late afternoon, but I didn't know if it was the day after the battle or even later. I felt completely disoriented, but I knew that the front line must have moved and I was totally on my own. They had left me there for dead. Later I learned that they had even reported me as dead.

I waited for nightfall to try to get up. I noticed that my uniform was covered with dried blood, and by my side lay my rifle, a carbine. I was ready to attempt to get up although I was not at all sure that I would succeed. It worked. Slowly, carefully, with the help of my rifle, I made it to my feet. How, I can't tell. I felt very wobbly on my legs, but I didn't fall. I took one step forward and it worked! The next one . . . the next one . . . and again . . . . I had made a number of steps when suddenly somebody fired at me and called out in German, "Stop! Who goes?"

I screamed out in German, "A wounded Polish legionnaire!"

The Austrian soldiers, our allies, believed me and helped me get over the trench. Then they laid me down and told me that they would send me back with the next field kitchen. When it arrived, they placed me in the back of the horse-drawn wagon in a sitting position with my legs dangling off the end. As the wagon bumped along, the pain became so acute that I asked the driver to stop and made the rest of the journey on foot, still in great pain, supporting myself on the side of the wagon.

After about half an hour, I reached brigade headquarters. As soon as I entered the building, I realized that I was in the room of the brigade commander and his doctor, Colonel Rogalski. When the brigade commander saw that I was only a non-commissioned officer, he told me brusquely that the hospital was at the other end of the village. If I had been stronger, I would have told them both what I thought of them, but being in such a weakened state I decided to try to reach the end of the village.

Somehow I succeeded.

When I reached the hospital, I fell down and couldn't move my limbs. I was in unimaginable pain as I was placed on a hospital train. They had to cut off my shoes and found that both my feet were frostbitten. The cold had staunched the flow of blood and actually helped to save my life! The hospital train was a converted cattle train with two rows of wooden bunks. After a few days it arrived at the military hospital where I spent almost half a year, including the Christmas holidays. Heavily wounded soldiers like me filled the hospital.

Next to my bed lay a young soldier with terrible wounds to his groin. I had to listen to the man's dreams of his young wife while he endured horrible pain having his dressings changed. He was so full of hope and optimism that he would be cured and return home, a subject to which he returned over and over again. The rest of us were speechless and full of sympathy; all of us knew that he would never be able to father children.

To a young man, this fate seemed worse than death!

In the spring, having recuperated from my stomach wounds, I returned to the Russian front. The fighting was as fierce as ever. This time I was responsible for rear-guard action as my battalion planned to move back. I watched wave after wave of the attacking Russians jump over a wooden fence, only to be mowed down by our bullets. Instead of crawling under that fence the way they should have, their officers made them jump over it, giving us perfect targets. As each new wave of men came over, they fell to the ground or hung on the fence, but their attack continued.

Forgetting that they were enemies, I felt sorry for them and thought, "What a barbaric waste of lives."

In spite of the enormous enemy losses, their numerical superiority decided the battle in their favor: Our officers ordered us to fall back to the edge of the woods.

Here I experienced an unexpected reaction from deep within my subconscious. Realizing the danger I faced, and remembering the horrible wounds of the soldier in the bed next to me in the military hospital, I thought to myself, I have to prevent a similar wound! While my comrades and subordinates fell back in proper military style, leapfrogging, I walked backwards, having taken off my backpack to hold it below my belt line.

During these moments I had no awareness that, in fact, I was exposing myself to even greater risk of being shot.

Luckily I reached the woods unharmed and only then did I realize how foolishly and unnecessarily I had exposed myself to further serious wounds or death. The criticisms of my buddies helped me reach this critical opinion of myself. I heard a quiet voice saying in the background, "What nonsensical bravery." I started to laugh, thinking, "It is not bravery as some may think, it is an insane fear — not cowardice — some sort of primeval prejudice that led me to this nonsensical reaction... I wanted an heir, and they thought that I was just showing off!"

--Memoirs of Julian S. Kulski

His memoir reveals my father — who always appeared omnipotent, larger-than-life, and heroic to me — as very human, honest, and self-critical. This anecdote of war, combining courage with human foibles, endears this man, an epitome of integrity, to his son.

Some inheritances are far more precious than wealth. When I say that I was born with a silver spoon in my mouth, I refer not to social privileges and financial means, but to the legacies and influences of courageous people of action like my father and grandmother and Norbert Barlicki. Though estranged from Aunt Stacha, my father's sister, Norbert could do no wrong in Father's eyes. My father's mother also loved Norbert. The three of them — Norbert, Father, and my grandmother — had worked together in the underground movement against the tsar during the Russian occupation. My grandmother, although in serious financial difficulty, had published an underground paper to spread the word about the movement against the tsar.

Summer Vacation

In August of 1939, our family went to Kazimierz, a resort near Warsaw on the Vistula River. Kazimierz was an historically Jewish river-port town famous for its ancient marketplace and for its synagogue, churches, and other medieval buildings. We stayed, as we had on previous holidays, at the Filipkowskis' boardinghouse, which was set amid varied and beautiful trees on a grassy hillside between the river and the town center.

I liked playing with Jedrek, the Filipkowskis' youngest son, and I was delighted to find Zula, my girlfriend at school, staying there with her family, too. The weather was splendid, and we enjoyed going for walks and swimming in the Vistula.

On Fridays the old town square was filled with pigs and chickens, wagons and mangy horses. Peasant women wearing colorful scarves on their heads perched on the wagons selling their goods to black-clad Orthodox Jews, the babble of Polish and Yiddish mixing with the cackling and squealing of the animals. Friday evenings, after the wagons had left and peace returned to the town, the Jews began celebrating their Sabbath in rooms lit by candles. Through the windows of the synagogue, we could see and hear men in long black robes and skullcaps bowing and praying in loud voices.

We had been at Kazimierz only a short time when a car came with a letter from Stefan Starzynski, the Lord Mayor of Warsaw, ordering my father to return to the capital at once. Father feared that Germany might attack Poland, and he said that we should stay in Kazimierz until he returned or sent for us. I told him that I wanted to go with him to fight as I didn't want to miss the war! He told me I was too young and that I should look after Mother and my sister, Wanda. I argued, but he stood firm.

Disappointed and frustrated, I got into mischief. Jedrek and I caught as many frogs as we could and threw them into our well, which caused a satisfying uproar among the adults. Then I made little Wanda cry, and that further helped release my pent-up anger. Finally, I ran away from home for awhile to spite my mother because I held her totally responsible for not letting me go. I knew that my father felt proud of me for wanting to fight. Surely if it had been up to him alone, Father would have allowed me to return with him.

A week later, I went walking in the woods, picking mushrooms with Zula. We spotted a white eagle hovering lazily over the deep gorge. Yes, we really saw a white eagle, the symbol of Poland! I knew these eagles were rare birds, and I was totally absorbed watching it. Suddenly, the bird disappeared, and I heard the deafening roar of engines overhead. As the huge planes with black crosses flew over the treetops, the woods filled with frightening wind and noise. The trees actually bent down, and I hit the ground absolutely terrified.

As soon as the phantom aircraft had vanished, I ran back to town with Zula. Mother was worried about Father. She said those were German planes, probably on their way to bomb Warsaw, flying low to avoid Polish antiaircraft defenses. That invasion, on September 1, 1939, marked the beginning of World War II.

Ten days later, the German planes bombed our medieval town, and some buildings caught fire. Many people fled to the woods with food and bedding, and I was very scared. Mother couldn't tell me whether this was happening all over

Poland or just in Kazimierz, and I wished I could ask Father.

On September 15, German troops arrived in Kazimierz looking bedraggled, dirty, and tired, looking nothing like victors. Their dusty, dark green uniforms and helmets weren't bright and beautiful like those of my toy soldiers. I wasn't impressed, and I was sure we would win the war.

A couple days later, the Germans tied the rabbi to the roof of the synagogue and set it afire. They taunted his congregation, telling them to go in and save him. I was so horrified that I ran away, but I couldn't outrun the memory, which still haunts me.

The same day Russia, secretly an ally of Germany, attacked the Polish Army from behind, along our eastern border. Poor Poland!

The New Order.

Part II

Germany Takes Over

The Shock of Surrender

A month after he left us, my father returned in a black Packard limousine to take us back to Warsaw. He looked haggard with fatigue, and he was limping. On the way, he told us about the capitulation of Warsaw on September 28. On that day remnants of the valiant Polish Army entered Krasinski Square in the heart of the Old City. Wounded and exhausted soldiers marched to the foot of the statue of Kilinski, the legendary hero of a long-ago uprising, which by some miracle was still standing. In the middle of the square, our soldiers laid down their arms. A few civilians stood by watching in tears.

Our country was the first to fall to the German army's strategy of *blitzkrieg* — attacking with overwhelming force and speed. When we reached the city, I saw skeletons of burned-out buildings and carcasses of dead horses. Dead bodies lay everywhere. Buildings still standing had empty, shattered windows. Our own house in Zoliborz had lost half its roof where a bomb fell. The glass was gone from all the windows, and the floors were covered with dust and slivers of glass that crunched under our feet. Our houseplants had died, and all my pets were gone save Skut, who had been with us. Except for the cold wind blowing steadily through the rooms, it was eerily silent. This was not the kind of war I had dreamed of in which we were the victors!

A few days later, against my mother's orders, I went to see my girlfriend Zula. Her family lived near Lazienki Park, the city's most beautiful park with its many flowers and a dramatic statue of our beloved Polish composer, Frederic Chopin. When I reached Zula's building, I rang the bell, not knowing whether her family had been marched off like many others. Zula let me in, and we went upstairs to her apartment. She said that an hour earlier the Germans had gone up and down the streets ordering all windows to be closed and all blinds drawn. Anyone seen on a balcony or looking through a window would be shot without warning.

We watched Hitler's victory parade from Zula's apartment. It was a parade for Germans only. I remember peeking through the curtain, wondering if they really would shoot anyone they spotted at a window. Tanks with their crooked crosses, called swastikas, sent shivers up my spine. German officers raised their hands high shouting "Heil Hitler!" to salute their leader, who stood at attention. There was Adolf Hitler, the Fuehrer himself, in the street below gloating over the destruction and death he had brought to my country. To me, he looked small and insignificant. I hated the Germans, but somehow his appearance did not inspire fear in me.

The Germans had imposed a curfew: Everyone had to be off the streets by dark. Soon I left Zula to get home before curfew. I made my way through deserted streets and caught the streetcar, feeling more determined than ever to participate in this war.

That was October 5, 1939, and we had no idea what we faced.

We got an idea a few days later when we listened to the radio broadcast of Hitler's speech in Berlin. He boasted about victory, about how Poland had tried his patience too long, about how the German-Russian Pact would obliterate Poland. Hitler raved like a madman about his solution to the "Jewish Problem" and how the Aryan master race would conquer all Europe even if Britain's Prime Minister Winston Churchill opposed him.

Norbert Barlicki came by whenever he could, bringing the latest proclamations and news of the tightening German Occupation. Uncle Norbert's head was massive, and his hair was always in disarray. His weathered face had bushy eyebrows and mobile facial expressions, and his eyes twinkled or frowned or smiled with every breath. I adored him.

Usually Uncle Norbert's deep voice boomed with resounding *joie de vivre*, but on these visits he and my father spoke in low, intense voices. Sometimes I managed to listen to them. It was never good news, and I hung onto every word. One night, Uncle Norbert and Father talked about a proclamation in the *New Warsaw Courier*, the daily newspaper that the Germans had taken over. The newly appointed Governor General, Hans Frank, had issued a proclamation ordering that all Poles, ages 18 to 60, be forced to labor in agriculture, road construction, or building waterways and railroads. Our people were to be slaves working to help the Germans conquer the rest of Europe!

There was more. The proclamation forbade cruelty to animals, which sounded fine to me, but it went on to define as cruel the killing of animals "for the purpose of the so-called kosher consumption of meats." The punishment for anyone who slaughtered meat according to kosher ritual, or who helped anyone who did, was "at least one year in a maximum-security prison..." and that punishment could "... also be carried out in concentration camps."

I had kept quiet, but at that point I interrupted to ask, "I can understand what the first part means, but not the last. Does it mean that Jews will not be able to get meat to eat?"

"Exactly," said Uncle Norbert. "We are beginning to see the first phase of the German Occupation Policy. Unfortunately, there will be more. I hate to think about what will follow."

In late October, the German secret police, the dreaded Gestapo, arrested Lord Mayor Stefan Starzynski, a good friend of my father. Starzynski and Father had had a chance to escape from Poland at the time of the German invasion. Other

Polish leaders had urged them to fly to the safety of London and work in the Polish government-in-exile. A plane had actually been sent from Romania to Warsaw to rescue them, but both men refused to be treated differently from the rest of Warsaw's citizens. Hitler was furious when Lord Mayor Starzynski spoke ardently in public radio announcements about the situation in Warsaw, especially in a broadcast that told the whole world how the Germans were bombing hospitals and killing civilians. We knew Hitler was taking revenge when Starzynski was arrested.

The Poles saw my father, the deputy mayor, as the natural successor of Starzynski as Lord Mayor of the nation's capital, and indeed Father moved into that office and assumed those responsibilities. But the Germans demoted him to *burgomeister*, a mere town mayor.

Our family had often hidden Polish soldiers and other displaced persons looking for safety in the city, but that day we made sure our house was "clean." We knew it would be watched closely from now on.

No School!

One morning in late November, I made my way through bombed-out streets past apartment houses whose front walls had been shorn off precisely as if by a huge knife. I could look into the open rooms and see the furniture and wallpaper. As I approached my school, I saw posted on the door a big notice announcing, "By order of the German authorities, all schools are closed."

What great news! I was elated.

With the schools closed, I had plenty of free time and finally could do whatever I wanted. The Germans had issued new postage stamps, which I spent time adding to my stamp album even though it made me angry to see that the German eagle had been overlaid on Polish stamps. Why did they have to ruin our beautiful stamps? Wasn't there anything they could leave alone?

Although my parents made me take some classes in secret schools organized in private homes, I still had time to visit Zula and to play with other boys my age. Some of us boys began our own private war against the Germans. We sneaked up to various street corners and tore down wooden signboards directing traffic to various German offices and military headquarters. With difficulty, I carried away some signs from Zoliborz street corners on my bicycle, being careful not to be seen by military or police patrols. The next day a lot of German trucks and cars could be seen roaming the streets wasting time and precious gasoline. Sometimes, a driver would stop and ask me for directions. I made sure to send him completely

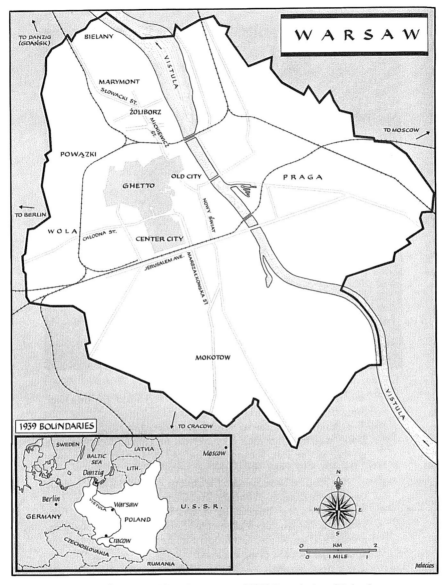

Map of Warsaw with an insert map of 1939 Boundaries of Poland.

the wrong way. The Germans quickly put up new signs, cursing the Poles, and we'd daringly repeat our trick after curfew.

In an even more dangerous prank, my best friend, Jedrek, and I picked up unexploded small bombs and shells on the streets, put them in my wagon and took them to his house. We disarmed these "dud" bombs, took out the explosive powder and made large firecrackers. We carefully placed our firecrackers between the tracks of streetcars in Zoliborz and hid in the bushes to wait. When a firecracker exploded and lifted the streetcar slightly from the tracks, the passengers screamed in fear and we were overjoyed. This was fun, more like what I expected the war to be — exciting, thrilling, and challenging. I was beginning to enjoy the adrenaline rush of danger.

As mayor, Father issued an appeal to the city's population to be careful of the dud shells strewn on the streets and parks because even though they hadn't exploded on impact, they still could go off. I didn't tell him what I had been doing with Jedrek — or that I was planning to get a gun.

The Division of Warsaw

By the end of November the newspapers were filled with the latest German orders: All Polish Jews had to wear a yellow armband with the Star of David on it. I wondered if the Germans would order us Christian Poles to wear an armband with a cross on it.

I continued to explore the city when I wasn't in the secret classes that my parents insisted I attend. The streets were full of movement during the day, but at curfew they were deserted and quiet except for the sound of German boots and police sirens. That shrieking noise and the random searches of homes turned Warsaw into a city of terror. By the middle of December, it was getting more difficult to see Zula. Our house had filled up with relatives and their servants from all over the country, so she couldn't come to visit me. Every time I went to see her, there was another new person in her house, too. Zula was edgy and cried easily, but she wouldn't tell me what was troubling her. I guessed that she and her mother still had no news of Zula's father, a Polish Army officer who had been taken prisoner in September 1939.

In April 1940, the newspapers carried the first hints that the Jews would be separated from the rest the city. In an interview, a German health director claimed that the Jews had to be isolated because they were carriers of typhus, a highly infectious and deadly disease.

In the middle of May, I went to the Old City and noticed that the rubble from bombed buildings around Bonifraterska Street was being used to build a huge wall. I wondered what was going on. The Germans were rounding up people they found suspicious and taking them off in enclosed trucks. By then, the Germans usually lumped all Poles together, Christians and Jews alike, describing our entire nation as being "subhuman," beneath their own "master race," the Aryans.

In October, when I tried to get to Zula's apartment in central Warsaw, the streets were roped off and I had to turn back. On October 12, on my way home through Zoliborz, I heard the public address speakers in Zeromski Park suddenly blare. Everyone came to a halt as the voice announced the division of the city into three separate and distinct housing areas: for Germans, for Polish Christians, and for Polish Jews. Families considered by the Germans to belong to one group but not living in the part of town assigned to their group had to leave their homes and move into the newly designated areas by the end of the month. People were shocked and frightened.

The Germans began forcing Jews — or anyone they suspected of being Jewish — to live in a so-called "Jewish residential district." This district included a part of town that had been called by the Italian term "ghetto" in medieval times, when Jews had been segregated from Christians throughout most of Europe. Such forced segregation had been abolished in Poland hundreds of years earlier, but this newly defined district did include a neighborhood of Orthodox Jews who maintained all the traditions of their community. Many less-traditional Jews lived and worked in the rest of Warsaw, indistinguishable from other Poles. And many Christian Poles had Jewish relatives or ancestors.

I couldn't believe it when they ordered Zula and her family to this new Ghetto. They were Catholic and her father was a Polish Army hero, but Zula had a Jewish grandparent. The Germans considered anyone "within three generations of Jewish blood" to be Jewish.

I visited Zula in the Ghetto a few times. It was heartbreaking to see dozens of people crowded into apartments meant for six or eight inhabitants. There wasn't enough food, and the Germans were hunting Jews on the streets like predators after game.

Towards the end of October, the *New Warsaw Courier* carried the names of the boundary streets for the Jewish residential district. I roamed around the city, on foot and by streetcar. By the time I had walked around the area that would constitute the Ghetto, I was dead tired. The Germans were walling in a huge part of the city! It made a solemn contrast to the bustling, lively area that I remembered from previous visits. People of all ages were pushing carts full of their belongings, jostling each other, their nerves on edge with fear.

By the middle of November the wall was finished. It had ten heavily guarded gates. Anybody entering or leaving was questioned and searched at gunpoint by guards who held attack dogs on short leashes. The guards and dogs both looked fierce.

Zula's Birthday

It puzzled me that the city streetcars still ran through the Ghetto on the old tracks. I decided to ride one, an unnerving experience. The streetcars entered the Ghetto at one gate and proceeded through the crowded streets at full speed without stopping. On each car was a member of the Polish "Blue" Police, charged with seeing that nobody jumped on or off the moving vehicles in the Ghetto.

Zula's birthday fell on a bitterly cold day, December 12, 1940, and she called to let me know that her family had finished moving. She gave me the address, and I went to visit her in the Ghetto. At the time, I didn't think about the risks involved. I just had to go see Zula, especially on her birthday. I had formulated a strategy to get inside the wall. I sat in the last seat of the streetcar, and I waited for the right opportunity. It happened close to Muranow Square, inside the Ghetto. Just as the streetcar slowed to turn the corner, the Blue policeman came from the streetcar's platform into the compartment to warm his hands. He walked past me, and while his back was turned, I quickly left the compartment and jumped off the metal step of the platform, disappearing into the crowd.

I made my way to the address that Zula had given me. The sidewalks and streets were hives of pushing, shoving humanity. People were pushing carts of bedding and furniture, searching for a place to call home. It was bedlam.

Zula and her mother seemed pleased that I had come, but Zula didn't talk much; she just kept looking at me with sad, dark eyes. Her mother tried to be optimistic, talking about how nice it was to find such a good place with friends. They lived in one room of an apartment owned by a widow whose brother-in-law, a lawyer, lived in another room with his two nephews. They all shared the kitchen and bathroom. The lawyer, a man of about thirty, joined us for a frugal supper of tea and bread. He said kindly that he'd heard a lot about me from Zula and was happy to have me with them. He told us there were now more than a quarter of a million people in this part of the city, but only 140,000 rooms. Such crowded conditions would cause sanitation problems and illness. He was especially outraged that the Germans were forcing all these people in here as a measure of "health protection" claiming, falsely, that Jews carried typhus.

The young lawyer was working for the newly formed Jewish Council headed by Adam Czerniakow, an engineer. Before the war Czerniakow had been a highly respected senator in the Polish Parliament and a member of the Warsaw Civic Council. I knew that my father had high regard for this outstanding Polish patriot.

As chairman of the Jewish Council, Adam Czerniakow was the Ghetto's unofficial mayor. He had complained repeatedly to various authorities about the overcrowding, starvation-level diet, lack of fuel for heating and cooking, and unsanitary conditions. But things only got worse. The young lawyer said the Germans were not only walling off the Jews from the rest of the city but also denying them their rights as Polish citizens.

Zula's mother was sure Czerniakow would work things out. "If anybody can handle the situation, it is Adam Czerniakow. He is not afraid of anybody — including the Germans. I understand they call him 'that fresh Jew' because he is not taking any nonsense from them." Czerniakow would often stand up to the Germans in defense of the Jews and be badly beaten. He had over his desk in the Ghetto a portrait of Marshal Pilsudski. The Germans made him take it down, surprised that a Jew would display a portrait of a Christian leader. They couldn't understand that Pilsudski was a hero to all Poles.

Darkness was falling, and curfew hour approached. I excused myself and after an affectionate goodbye to Zula, I jumped on the last streetcar leaving the Bonifraterska Street Gate. Fortunately, it was empty, and there was no police guard. At home that night I found it impossible to sleep. My mind kept turning over what I had seen and heard. It was no wonder my father was increasingly despondent every time Adam Czerniakow came to City Hall. Father secretly helped many people, but he couldn't make the Germans do anything.

Father had been interrogated several times but remained the mayor, in charge at City Hall. The Germans hadn't figured out that City Hall was actually a headquarters for the Polish underground resistance movement, which couldn't have existed without Father's help in providing false identification papers, cover stories, and hiding places. A great number of the people officially listed as employees of City Hall were rarely there because their real work was organizing resistance groups in the city and around the country. Under constant observation by the Gestapo, Father earned the nickname "Prisoner of the City Hall" among Poles who knew what a dangerous double life he was leading.

The next day, to distract myself from thoughts of what was happening to Zula, I went to see my chemistry-wizard friend, Jedrek. We had had fun making firecrackers and putting them under streetcars. This time I agreed to help him build a small arsenal of real weapons. We resumed our search for dud artillery shells, hauling them back to his house and storing the gunpowder in jam jars in his garage. Jedrek lived far enough away from my house that I thought my parents would never find out about our playing with explosives in our "laboratory."

A few days before Christmas, Jedrek got his hands on something we really needed — nitroglycerine. We knew that this semi-liquid substance was an important ingredient of bombs, but we had no idea how it should be handled or that it could explode if dropped. We worked from early morning until late afternoon dividing the nitro and putting it in test tubes for storage. I had to get home before curfew, and Jedrek said he would wait for my return before carrying on. He promised to lock up and go to his room.

In all the excitement, I'd forgotten to ask him where he'd gotten the nitro. I figured I could ask him the next day, but it snowed heavily all night, and the morning dawned fiercely cold and clear. I planned to go to Jedrek's garage around noon, but at midmorning a neighbor arrived with news of a terrible explosion. I grabbed my jacket and ran as fast as I could to our laboratory. The garage was a shambles, and Jedrek had been taken to the hospital. The blast nearly killed my buddy. Once again, I was lucky. If I had been there, it's a safe bet that I would have been hurt or killed. After Jedrek's arm was amputated, I gave up this dangerous project of manufacturing weapons.

Christmas 1940

Zula's situation and my friend's accident put me in a dark mood for Christmas. I took little part in the family activities. Mother tried to cheer us up. As in past years when she had taught Wanda and me to waltz, she wanted all of us to dance. She had scrounged and saved for weeks preparing for this occasion. I noticed that she no longer wore her beautiful diamond ring. She wouldn't admit it, but I was sure she had sold it to get money for food. She had gone from being a woman of means, with servants and a governess, to selling her jewelry on the black market. I didn't appreciate her fully at the time, but she was a true soldier in her own way.

Our Christmas tree seemed the most beautiful we'd ever had, its candles reflected in the glistening ornaments. As on all special occasions, Father read aloud stories from the works of Charles Dickens and Mark Twain, in Polish translation. We exchanged gifts, greetings, and embraces, and we broke the communion wafer to share the spirit of Christ. But something was lacking.

The traditional empty chair that year was for Uncle Norbert. We had heard nothing from him since summer, when he had been taken to Pawiak Prison.

I couldn't shake my melancholy, so I left them all — Mother, Father, Wanda, aunts, the many "guests" who now made their home with us, the maids, and our little dachshund, Skut — and retired to the solitude of my room.

Early in January 1941, we learned that Uncle Norbert was among five hundred prisoners moved from Pawiak Prison to unheated cattle cars at Warsaw West station. The trains were headed out of the city toward the German concentration camp of Auschwitz near the Polish city of Krakow. The Germans had taken my favorite uncle, and his chances of survival were slim. I wanted to shout, to scream, above all to fight! But all we could do at that point was to wait.

It was getting harder to control our fears. A few nights later I woke up to the screaming of sirens. The Gestapo seemed to be arresting people all over our Zoliborz neighborhood. After I fell asleep again, I had a nightmare in which Uncle Norbert appeared and stood by my bed. He looked haggard, sick and lonely. His eyes seemed to plead with me: "Come and help me. Get me out of this place, Julek. Get me out!"

My father lived each day in great peril. As Mayor of Warsaw, he had to wear two faces, one for the Germans and the other for the Poles, whom he continued to help in countless forbidden ways. I remember vividly one time when the Germans came to search our house and arrested him. Wanda flew into hysterics, and I put my arms around her and calmed her down. Father was often taken hostage for days by the German military authorities or arrested and interrogated by the Gestapo and then released, narrowly escaping a one-way ticket to Auschwitz or, more likely, the execution squad in nearby Palmiry Woods.

In March, right after my 12th birthday, my father had a serious chat with me when he discovered that I had been hiding a pistol in the attic, a Colt 45 automatic. What with Father's frequent arrests and his being out of the house most of the time, he believed that I would be better off with somebody else looking after me. Basically, it boiled down to this: Either I would get my father in trouble, or my father would get me in trouble. I told him that I understood, and that I wanted to go into the woods to join the Polish partisans and fight the Germans. I saw pride in my father's deep blue eyes, but he told me that I would have to wait a little longer.

That's all I ever heard while growing up: "when you are a little older." I could do what I wanted when I was older, have sex when I was older, fight the Germans when I was older. I got sick and tired of hearing it.

I couldn't even visit Zula now. They had closed all the gates to the Ghetto, and the streetcars had been re-routed outside the wall. For many reasons, but especially for the sake of Uncle Norbert and Zula, I felt a rising tide of passion to join the fight against our oppressors.

Ludwik Berger — 1942.

Part III

Underground Army

Living with Ludwik

A month after my father said I'd be safer living with someone else, I moved into the house of my pre-war scoutmaster, Ludwik Berger, and my life changed radically. My new home was a small, pleasant, sunny attic room above Ludwik's second-floor apartment three blocks from my parents' house on Felinski Street.

I had missed Boy Scout activities since the war began and had wondered what my beloved scoutmaster was doing. Ludwik, a well-known actor and theater producer, was an imposing, handsome giant, six feet six inches tall, with an eagle's nose and dark wavy brown hair. Adding to his dramatic appearance, he wore a long belted coat and Polish Army boots. I remember capturing his image on film with my little camera. He had a commanding voice and excellent diction and knew many poems by heart. I loved to listen to his melodious voice as he recited them with dramatic flair.

The apartment was home to Ludwik, his girlfriend, Stefa Sokal, her sister Aleksandra (known as Ola), their grandmother, and Ludwik's eight-year-old son, Marek. Stefa was intellectual in her interests and devoted to Ludwik and his son. Ola, who was more athletic, had taught physical education at a high school for girls before the war. When the Germans had invaded in 1939, she had shown great bravery in the defense of Warsaw, going into the trenches to dress the wounds of Polish soldiers.

I didn't know it at the time, but all the people in the apartment had Jewish ancestry, and I'm sure my father knew this. Sometimes ignorance is protection. If the Germans had asked me whether the people I lived with were Jewish, I would have said no in all sincerity. All I knew was that Mother thought highly of Dr. Sokal, father of Stefa and Ola, because he had been her father's physician. And Ludwik's mother, like my mother's family, came from the city of Lwow.

For the same reason, Father chose not to tell me that I, too, have Jewish ancestry. Father's grandmother was the daughter of a rabbi. Neither her family nor her husband's had approved the match, and the rabbi from then on denied ever having a daughter. According to the Germans' arbitrary definition — within three generations — Father would have been classified as Jewish but I would not. Not knowing this family history, I was spared a lot of the fear that he must have felt as the Germans' desire to eliminate all Jews became more and more clear.

Soon after moving into his building, I learned that Ludwik had organized a group of underground resistance fighters in the Zoliborz neighborhood as soon as the Germans took over Warsaw. His group consisted mostly of former Boy Scouts and Girl Scouts and a few pre-war army officers who had escaped from

German POW (Prisoner of War) camps. Everybody in the company underwent strict military training, and Ludwik kept busy arming his scouts in all sorts of ways. He bought weapons, stole weapons, and unearthed still more weapons that had been buried by Polish troops on the verge of surrender in 1939. Ludwik's soldiers learned to scavenge for weapons any place they could.

Father sent me to Ludwik on the trusted recommendation of Colonel Emil Kumor of the Polish underground army. Although he wanted me safe, I believe that my father knew well what path I would follow under Ludwik Berger's influence. Uncle Norbert had played a similar role in inspiring my father and other youngsters of his generation. In choosing Ludwik, Father sent me to the best place to fulfill my desire to fight the Germans.

In June 1941, I stopped by my home and overheard my parents whispering about Uncle Norbert, who had been sent to the Auschwitz concentration camp. Someone who had escaped from the camp said that Uncle Norbert was organizing an underground group there. Even sick, depressed, and weak, he was playing a leading role in the resistance movement—from inside Auschwitz! Other prisoners were doing everything possible to look after him. I prayed for him to survive, but reports of the dreadful conditions in that concentration camp made me fear for his life.

On July 12, Ludwik and I had a long talk. He revealed the existence of a secret military organization, the Union for Armed Resistance, and he asked whether I would like to join and fight the Germans. I was thrilled and, of course, accepted at once. That summer, at long last, the war started in earnest for me when I became a member of his company at age 12. A born leader of young people, Ludwik became my role model and my hero. I would have obeyed him even if he had not been my superior and the highest-ranking officer in the company.

Ludwik went all out to prepare me for the conspiratorial work of the underground army, emphasizing the obvious need for total secrecy and discipline. I was only 12 but grown up enough to understand the most important requirement of all: willingness to give one's life in the fight for freedom. I felt more than ready.

Secrecy and Discipline

Saturday, July 19, 1941, was one of the most important days in my life. That evening after curfew, Ludwik made me get my jacket and cap. We traversed the streets stealthily, avoiding the bright lights of the boulevards. I felt a thrill of anticipation as we made our way toward the Vistula River, at last reaching the protective cover of the Lower Park near the river's edge. A number of individuals materialized out of the shadows. I knew that I was about to meet members of the underground army face to face.

First, the password: "Honor."

Then the response: "Service."

One man stepped forward, stood to attention and reported, "Group ready to take oath, Sir."

Then Ludwik took over the command and ordered the group to form ranks. I realized then that I was not the only one about to take the oath. In the small square between rows of bushes, complete silence reigned. One could hear the rustling of leaves, and from time to time the lights of passing German vehicles flashed over the flood embankment. It was a spectacular night with a full moon.

The orders sounded: "Fall in. Dress by the Right. Attention. Prepare for the oath."

The line stood unmoving, each man bareheaded and making the double-fingered eye-level salute. Then, the words of the soldier's oath:

"In the presence of God Almighty, I swear that I will faithfully and to the end defend the honor of Poland. I will fight to liberate the country from slavery with all my strength, even to the sacrifice of my own life. I will obey all orders of the Union without reserve and will maintain complete secrecy whatever might happen to me."

Ludwik gave the classic response to the oath:

"I accept you into the ranks of the soldiers for freedom. Your duty will be to fight with arms in hand for the rebirth of your country. Victory will be your reward. Treason will be punished by death."

Silence again punctuated the darkness of this secret rendezvous, and we stood motionless, each of us dreaming the same dream – freedom and independence for Poland. The military order "Company, at ease!" brought us back to reality. After the order to fall out, we fighters for freedom dispersed under the cover of night, melting mysteriously into the darkness of the shrubbery.

The moment I took that oath, I lost my childhood innocence. I was a soldier. I would bear arms, kill or be killed by the enemy. I was dedicating my life to freeing Poland from the Germans. I was a boy no more.

Ludwik and I left the park like the others, covertly. The occasion transcended words. Neither of us spoke as we made our way home.

A few days later I attended my first secret gathering, where I learned about the rules of secrecy. Because capture and torture were distinct possibilities, we did not learn each other's true identities. Each of us chose his own alias, or code name, such as *Wilk* (Wolf), or *Boruta* (Devil). Some freedom fighters, using their imagination, called upon animals, places, battles, biblical or historical figures for inspiration in choosing a code name.

Ludwik's code names originated with his parents: *Goliat* (Goliath) had been his father's alias during World War I, and *Michal*, his other alias, came from his mother's name, Michalina. I took for my alias *Chojnacki*, the name of one of my uncles who had been taken prisoner by the Germans in 1939. I remembered Uncle Chojnacki, the father of my favorite cousin, wearing a particularly beautiful Polish Army uniform.

We learned the importance of always carrying "authentic" identity papers — official documents issued by City Hall with real or fake names depending on our mission. Without proper papers, we could be detained on a technicality that, in German-occupied Warsaw, could prove fatal. We were warned not to meet each other. We were to keep our sights on our goal: to get ready for the uprising, a mass revolt against the occupiers.

Our infantry training included special attention to the demands of urban fighting. From time to time, we practiced maneuvers outside the city to prepare us for forest warfare as well. I also received preparation for special work as a member of the Couriers Section, responsible for carrying secret messages between underground army officers.

Sections in the underground army were kept very small to maintain secrecy. My section had only five men besides our commander, Lance Corporal *Boruta* (Devil). Thin, tall, and round-shouldered with a hooked nose, his pseudonym suited him very well, for he looked a bit devilish. Our army's chain of command was organized in groups of three: three sections in a detachment, three detachments in a platoon, and three platoons in a company.

Our Couriers Section was in a detachment in the platoon called *Walecznych*, which means "brave". Our platoon was in the company named *Orzel* (Eagle), the symbol of Poland. Eagle Company, the very first company formed in the underground army, never had more than about 150 members. Sixty percent of them were in their teens. Fifteen to twenty percent of our company were young women who served in all areas, not only as nurses and cooks but also in the signals and couriers sections and as front-line fighters. One young teenaged girl was in charge of ammunition, weapons supplies, and maintenance. Ludwik Berger, Commandant *Michal* of Eagle Company, made me his courier.

It didn't take me long to grasp fully the profound meaning of the soldier's oath that I had sworn in the park. The pounding of my pulse that July night was mild compared with what was to come. I would soon discover what happens to someone who swears loyalty and then betrays that oath.

Trapping a Traitor

The underground resistance depended on secrecy. The loyalty of the freedom fighters had to be as natural and automatic as breathing. We viewed any breach in security as one more blow against Polish freedom, and treason was no joking matter among our ranks. If we suspected anyone of double-dealing, especially with the Gestapo, we had to determine where his true loyalties lay.

As Ludwik's courier, I was privy to many secrets. Living in his home, I found even myself under his scrutiny. Ludwik had everything to lose if I turned traitor. I knew I couldn't, wouldn't betray my people; treachery was against my upbringing, against all my principles and inheritance. But these were terrifying times, and I was tested, too. We all were.

One young fellow came under a cloud of suspicion. In a secret meeting, *Michal* (Ludwik) and a few of his top men entrusted me with a special assignment: To find out beyond a shadow of a doubt whether this fellow was loyal or a traitor.

Since the young man was suspected of being a Nazi collaborator, the best approach was to pretend that I, too, felt ready to join the Germans. I offered to find out the true identity of *Michal*, the underground thorn in the Gestapo's side. With enthusiasm, the suspect welcomed me and accepted my offer. We agreed to meet again and made plans for a secret rendezvous near the Citadel. I crept away in the dark.

Disillusioned and shocked, I reported immediately to *Michal* and his officers. They grilled me on the meeting with the suspected traitor. They wanted to know every word, every detail. It was very serious business, and although I was still only 12, I felt the last traces of boyish innocence fall from me like leaves from a tree in autumn, thinking as I did that I might be responsible for another human being's fate. What precisely happened I do not know, but that young man disappeared without a trace. I felt both compassion and shame for that poor fool who so easily sold out his commander and his country.

I'm still horrified by people who betray national secrets for a price. I'm equally appalled by the necessity of killing in order to settle disputes, and I hope to heaven that human beings may someday learn to live peacefully in spite of—and because of—our differences, be they ideological, theological, cultural, or political.

Uncle Norbert

Having Ludwik as my leader and role model helped me understand how Father felt about Uncle Norbert, who had been a freedom fighter 13 years his senior when Father was a teenager. My hero, Ludwik Berger, was 13 years older than I. Norbert excited the imagination and dreams of my father and many other future leaders of Poland who wanted to fight for the freedom and independence of the country, just as Ludwik's abilities and knowledge of Polish history excited my imagination. Ludwik actually made my dreams of becoming a freedom fighter a reality. We had a hidden cache of arms in Ludwik's apartment just as Norbert kept weapons hidden in my father's childhood home. We were both lucky, my father and I. Norbert Barlicki and Ludwik Berger were hyper-intelligent, rare men.

Many of Norbert's students recall him as an unkempt professor who never lectured from a book, but whose fiery speeches, ranging from politics to art history, left indelible marks on their lives. When father and his sister, Stacha, were young, Norbert tutored them at home. According to my father, Norbert was a born teacher, eloquent and inspirational, who not only educated but also helped to create a worldview and social consciousness among the young. He also shared his love of music and fine paintings.

Instead of being paid for his teaching, Norbert stayed as an unpaid guest in their apartment. Father's mother, like Norbert, was deeply involved in underground anti-Russian activities: conspiratorial press, arms dealings and other patriotic work. In 1910 Norbert and my father landed in the infamous Pawiak, the political prison in Warsaw. My father was 17 at the time. During that period prior to World War I, Norbert, who had a tremendous sense of humor, started to refer to my father and himself as "heroes" — only half in jest because he foresaw the heroic roles they would play when the chance came to win independence from Russia.

By the end of World War I, Russia was very weak, and the overthrow of its government in the Russian Revolution gave Poland that chance. During the Russo-Polish War of 1919-21, the Polish armies were at first victorious and pushed the Red Army beyond the Ukraine. But a new offensive by the Red Army brought the Russians all the way to the outskirts of Warsaw. Then the tide of war changed when Marshal Jozef Pilsudski led a successful counteroffensive. Russia's Red Army suffered unredeemed defeat in that Battle of Warsaw. The battle, sometimes called "the Miracle on the Vistula," was a great victory for Poland, and the Russians signed a peace treaty recognizing Poland's borders.

During the preparation for that battle, Marshal Pilsudski called together all the national leaders, including Norbert Barlicki, to present to them his strategy for the military defense of Warsaw. Upon hearing the marshal's strategic plan, Norbert dared to question him about it. The marshal bristled at being questioned by a non-military man and replied, "This is what Napoleon Bonaparte would propose in this situation." My dear Uncle Norbert looked around the room and replied with relish and a disarming smile, "But I do not see Napoleon at this table!" Ever the rebel, Norbert Barlicki couldn't help challenging powerful people, even Polish leaders.

Pilsudski never liked Barlicki after that. In 1931, as the head of state of independent Poland, Pilsudski arrested the leaders of all the political parties that opposed him and sent them to prison. Norbert Barlicki received the longest sentence, two and a half years.

In July 1940, Father and Uncle Norbert saw each other in Warsaw's Pawiak Prison yet again. Norbert, spotting my father among the arrested national leaders, murmured to him, "Heroes meet again." They spent four days in the same cell. That was the last time Father saw Norbert before the Germans shipped him to Auschwitz. Norbert was one of the first national leaders sent to that concentration camp. We worried about how a man of 60 could survive the extremely harsh conditions there. We had already heard rumors of his underground activities in the camp. If we knew, the Gestapo knew. Norbert stood out anywhere, even in a prison camp, and he remained dedicated to fighting for Poland's freedom throughout his imprisonment.

On October 15, 1941, a telegram arrived with the dreaded announcement that Norbert had died. No details were offered, not even the date of his death. My parents and I felt stunned and heartbroken. We had hoped that Uncle Norbert would somehow survive and be free again. I had been at home visiting with my mother when we got the news. I went to my Aunt Stacha's room. She was polishing the furniture, obviously in shock.

"Uncle Norbert is dead," I said, crying.

My aunt did not respond. Her face was expressionless, and her eyes seemed empty. She continued dusting, moving about silently as if I weren't there. I sat quietly for a while, then left, going out alone. I felt as if the whole world were crumbling about me. Despondent and utterly miserable, I could not believe that Uncle Norbert was gone.

A few weeks later, a friend of Uncle Norbert's delivered an envelope for Aunt Stacha. It contained some of Norbert's papers and the information that he had died of a "heart attack" in Auschwitz. The Germans claimed that everyone who died at Auschwitz had had a heart attack, but we knew they had been murdered.

At Christmastime, I left Ludwik's apartment and went back to Felinski Street to spend the holidays with my family. On Christmas Day, my Aunt Stacha refused to eat dinner, but she called me to her room and handed me an envelope. She said it was from my Uncle Norbert and that she wanted me to keep it in remembrance of him. I waited until after dinner and went to my room to open the envelope. In it was a poem written by my uncle, one of the last that he wrote.

> I could hasten death
> And run away from the field
> Where fear tears apart the last lights –
> I wait, however.
> Let fate run its course.
> The soul will not be dishonored
> In the ashes of fear.
> After my death, from the lonely grave
> I wish a bitter flower would grow
> And again look proudly
> To the clouds of misfortune,
> To the changeable heights,
> Proving there is no penance
> In my coffin.

> I am alone!
> I cry in vain,
> Alone and helpless
> Like a dried-up leaf.
> The winds of the desert
> Are carrying me.
> I am dying!
> Heart, have courage
> In this final tribulation.

Always considerate, loving, and generous in his lifelong pursuit of truth and beauty, my uncle was a poet and artist at heart. I felt a terrible tightening in my chest, as though I would burst. Then I wept.

Mission to the Ghetto

But there was little time for crying. By February 1942 the underground press announced that the underground army had reached organizational strength far beyond what was required for mere resistance operations. General Sikorski reorganized the Union for Armed Resistance (known by the Polish initials ZWZ) into the Home Army (the AK, for *Armia Krajowa*). The focus of the Home Army was the war of liberation, culminating in a nationwide uprising.

Ludwik informed me that our group of freedom fighters, Eagle Company, had grown to become a Home Army battalion called BASZTA, the initials of the Polish words for Battalion of the General Staff. What had been Ludwik's private army, his Scouts, now had to follow rules and orders from above his level. Our training was stepped up, and Ludwik again spared no efforts to acquire arms for his soldiers. New recruits came in all the time, many of them in their late teens and twenties. They came from various backgrounds but worked together without regard for social class or wealth. Their zeal, patriotism, youth, and singleness of purpose were my inspiration. I just hoped that I wouldn't let them down. I felt determined to show them that we younger boys, the former Boy Scouts, could fight like men.

Also that February my mother told me that the underground leadership again asked my father to get on a plane and fly to the safety of London, where a Polish government-in-exile represented our country during the German Occupation. Father refused. He felt that he could best serve the people of Warsaw by staying in Poland. He continued to blatantly disobey the unjust laws so brutally imposed on the city by the *Wehrmacht*, the German Army.

Most Poles resisted the Germans in every way they could. The underground army asked everybody to avoid giving any aid or comfort to our enemies and to save our money for essentials like food and for helping our freedom fighters prepare for an uprising. For example, we were asked not to waste money going to a movie, not to be friendly with Germans or to spend money in their shops or businesses, and to work as slowly as possible to delay German projects. On March 3, 1942, I celebrated my 13th birthday. My father managed to spend some time with me, but spent most of it speaking of his outrage at the order issued by the *Wehrmacht* to melt down all the city statues, supposedly because the Germans needed the metal for manufacturing tanks and other weapons. All our statues! Our heroes! Our very history was to be destroyed!

After months of behind-the-scenes maneuvers, Father finally went to see Ludwig Leist, his German overseer, and found that he, too, was furious about the

A Ghetto Child.

order because the *Wehrmacht* had issued it without his prior approval. Leist gave my father permission to have casts made of all the city's monuments so that after the war we could make exact replicas of the statues. That decision put a smile on my father's face. He figured it would take months, perhaps years, to accomplish this task. He would make darn sure the work went very slowly. And he did.

The Germans wanted more than metal from us. They took everything they could, especially food. My mother resorted to smuggling food from the country to the city, watching for police patrols at the stations. Whenever she spotted one, she threw the precious food out the windows of the train to avoid arrest and deportation to a concentration camp. "Black markets" (people secretly and illegally selling food and other things) flourished in Warsaw. The black-market prices were exorbitant and the risks enormous, but at least we had food. The Jews, trapped inside the Ghetto, were not able to take advantage of the black markets. Rumors from behind the wall ran to gruesome accounts of starvation and people dying in the streets.

My father told me that Adam Czerniakow, the head of the Jewish Council in the Ghetto, had come to his office in City Hall and bluntly asked him if he knew the fate of Jews being sent out of Warsaw in cattle cars. Father told him that he feared the Jews were being taken to their deaths. Having worked closely with Czerniakow since 1939, Father felt he would want the truth. Czerniakow replied that he doubted the two of them would survive the war.

On September 1, 1942, Ludwik said he wanted me to accompany him on a special mission into the Ghetto. If anything happened to him, I was instructed to return and report to our company. At the time I wondered: If something happens to him, won't it happen to me, too? However, I said nothing. I was completely terrified by the whole idea, but I concealed my fear. Secrecy had become an all-consuming way of life.

Not long after midnight, Ludwik and I made our surreptitious way to a house close to the Ghetto wall where we met the young Jewish man who served as our guide. He knew the secret way into and out of the Ghetto but could not share that precious knowledge with us. Blindfolded and literally led by the hand, we descended to the cellars and for what seemed like hours made our way along dark, subterranean passages. When they took our blindfolds off, we were dazzled at first by the daylight, and then saw that we were inside the Ghetto, near Mila Street. Our guide handed us over to two other young men who escorted us to the actual meeting place. They made us change into rags because our clothes were in such good condition that they would have betrayed us instantly as outsiders. The adrenaline of danger kept us going.

On the way to the meeting, I couldn't believe my eyes. Starving people looked like skeletons with sunken, glassy eyes. The dying lay on the ground or leaned against buildings. The stench of decomposing corpses assaulted us. That walk was a living nightmare. There didn't seem to be any old people, but everyone looked old. I saw children dying — right out in the open. Nothing I had heard or read prepared me for what I saw firsthand in the Ghetto.

At one point, we saw a solitary German soldier firing at random. People began running past us, and we watched a woman fall, shot in the stomach. Our guides dragged us into a doorway as the soldier continued to spray the street with bullets. When he saw that the rest of his targets had managed to get away, he turned back down Meisels Street (named after the national hero Rabbi Dob Beer Meisels, who I learned much later was my father's great grandfather). I had heard rumors that German soldiers on leave were hunting starving Jews on the streets of the Ghetto for sport, but until now I had not believed those stories. Ludwik appeared to be just as horrified by what we had seen.

Finally, we reached the meeting with members of the Jewish underground. They told us of their sufferings and asked us to get word to London and the rest of the world about the deportation of thousands of Jews that had begun in July. The Germans led people to believe that the conditions had become so crowded that some people were being sent to work in the country. Actually, they were being transported to extermination camps.

One of the Jewish freedom fighters then recounted the sad story of the death of the Ghetto's unofficial mayor, Adam Czerniakow. A few weeks after visiting my father's office, Czerniakow had written a desperate warning to his people: "Three p.m. So far, three thousand ready to go. By four p.m., according to orders, there must be nine thousand. I am helpless; sorrow and pity fill my heart. I cannot stand it any longer. My end will show everybody what must be done." He then killed himself.

Ludwik broke in to ask, "Did the people get the message?"

"The news of Czerniakow's death spread like fire. It was a clear-cut warning of the liquidation of Warsaw Jews. However, even now, most people refuse to believe the truth. The smell of fresh bread and the promise of three kilograms of bread and one of jam win them over. Starving people volunteer and line up to board the trains."

The talks were extensive and complex to a 13-year-old, but what I understood of them was so horrible that it terrified me: Of the 400,000 Jews living in the Ghetto in July, only about 100,000 remained. After an hour, the Jews asked Ludwik to have me wait in an adjoining room while they talked to him privately. In a depressing dark room, I sat for a long time filled with forebodings and fear. I kept wondering what had become of dear Zula and her family, but there was no way to find out. When Ludwik returned, he, too, looked frightened.

Ludwik and I spent the night in the Ghetto, but we talked very little. The next morning the meeting resumed. The Jewish underground wanted arms and ammunition to start an uprising. They admitted that they could not win, but, unified by the vicious aggression of the Germans, they wanted to die fighting for the future of the Jews.

On our way back to the other side of the wall, we saw homemade posters warning people not to board the trains going to extermination camps. The posters pleaded:

Hide your children! Hide yourselves!
Resist deportation!
Join the Resistance!
Don't die with a Torah in your hands!
Die with weapons in your hands!

The Ghetto Uprising

In April 1943, when a German force of more than 800 SS troops entered the Ghetto fortress to quell rumored unrest, the Jewish underground army attacked them, launching the uprising of the Warsaw Ghetto. By morning Polish and Jewish flags hung above the rooftop of an apartment house on Muranow Street. This sight stirred all of us in Warsaw. That evening our AK underground commandos blew an opening in the wall along Bonifraterska Street, giving vital access to besieged fighters in the adjacent street. Days later, when the Jewish freedom fighters rejected the German ultimatum to lay down arms and surrender, the Germans brought tanks, flame throwers, field artillery, and armored cars into the battle.

Assigned to Bonifraterska Street, I witnessed the battle. I was amazed that both sides — Germans and freedom fighters alike — held their fire every time a streetcar passed alongside the Ghetto! Hours later, when the streetcar to Bielany was waved through the fighting, a burst of Jewish machine-gun fire toppled three Germans. The crowd watching roared its approval, but the Germans, enraged, turned their guns on the crowd. Some people fell; others scattered.

More than 300 freedom fighters, including some Christian Poles, died in the Ghetto, which the German soldiers began to destroy systematically house by house. The Ghetto Uprising, however, revitalized the hopes of the city, and the Germans paid dearly in blood for every captured basement bunker. From all over Warsaw the flames of the burning Ghetto buildings were visible, proof of the bravery of the defenders, who raised a poster on the corner of Bonifraterska Street that proclaimed, "Long Live Freedom!"

Some survivors remained in the Ghetto's ruins, in bunkers the Jews had built before the uprising. Known as "Robinson Crusoes," they hid by day and threatened

Captured Freedom Fighters awaiting execution, 1943 Uprising.

German patrols by night. Many of these freedom fighters survived and continued to prepare for a national uprising. (It is a little-known fact that even more Jewish freedom fighters died in the later Warsaw Uprising than in the Ghetto Uprising. My company had Jewish members as did many other units. When the Polish forces capitulated, the surviving Jews stayed in Warsaw until the Russians took over.)

Pawiak Prison.

Part IV

Gestapo Prisoner

Pawiak Prison

In June 1943 the Gestapo net began to close in on Ludwik and the people living in his apartment. A wedding party of freedom fighters, betrayed by a traitor, was rounded up during the church ceremony downtown. The Gestapo hauled about 89 people to Pawiak Prison. The Germans found incriminating documents on several members of the wedding party. The prisoners were paraded through the courtyard of the prison while the traitor, hiding his face behind his hands, stood at a window pointing out key individuals of our underground army to the Gestapo.

Ludwik's girlfriend, Stefa, and I learned from his intelligence contacts that her sister, Ola, had been arrested at that wedding. Ola was carrying a gun, some papers, and her false identity card, all of which linked her to the underground. Taken with the others to the Gestapo headquarters, she was interrogated and refused to answer any questions. Neither threats nor beatings could break her. She was kicked, beaten, and later put on the rack, the torture machine that we called the "bed of death." By the time that last session of interrogation and torture ended, Ola knew she had reached her limit. Rather than break down and betray her comrades, when she returned to her cell she reached for the cyanide capsule concealed in her clothes and took the poison. Aleksandra Sokal, our beautiful Ola, remained silent until the end. When we heard this news, grief and pity overwhelmed me. Stefa broke down and wept bitterly.

I went to stay at my parents' house on Felinski Street but kept in touch with Stefa. A week later, I returned to the apartment. Ludwik was away, in hiding, and Stefa spoke little. She knew she was living on borrowed time. Her only consolation seemed to be eight-year-old Marek, Ludwik's little boy, playing with his toys on the floor.

At three o'clock, a knock on the door announced the arrival of the Gestapo. They pretended to be friendly, but Stefa knew better. She obeyed their order to open up. Ludwik had told me to escape capture if possible, so I ran to the next room to try to leap off the balcony. But the Gestapo shouted, *"Hande hoch!"* (Hands up!) I obeyed, raising my hands high, and turned. I was looking down the barrel of a machine gun. Quite frankly, I was scared stiff and certain that all was lost. They searched me from head to toe, then began a rapid search of the house. I knew immediately that they were looking for two things: Ludwik and arms.

Standing stone still, I looked sideways at Marek. He caught my glance and turned quickly away to focus on his menagerie spread out on the floor. The Gestapo split up. Two stayed behind with Marek, and the others ordered Stefa and me to leave. I took one last glance at Marek while we left the room. He was sitting on the secret trapdoor to our arms cache talking to his toy family spread out on the carpet. He looked at me, and as sunlight fell on his face I saw tears forming in his eyes.

We were escorted under armed guard out on the street to police cars, open Mercedes convertibles that took us to Szucha Avenue, the Gestapo headquarters. It took an hour for the officers there to complete their dossier on us. Then they took us in "Black Maria" vans to Pawiak Prison, located in the middle of the burned-out Ghetto. That area was under strict quarantine, and I saw only a few German guards amid the ruins. I finally admitted to myself that my beautiful girlfriend Zula was probably dead.

We passed a pack of wild, lean Alsatian dogs that snarled and bared their fangs. The convoy passed quickly through the second and last gate and braked to a halt in front of the reception center. They took Stefa to the women's section, me to the men's. A guard smashed me into a wall for moving my hand just a fraction, and I realized that what little freedom I had had a few hours earlier on the streets of Warsaw was now gone. I was totally at the mercy of the SS guards of Pawiak Prison.

They put me in a tiny cell filled to bursting with prisoners. Some had been arrested because of suspected Jewish ancestry. Others were jailed just for attempting to flee the city. The guards put me through a medical examination and confiscated my few belongings. To compound these indignities, they shaved my head; I minded that the most.

They led me to a six-feet-by-nine-feet basement cell and locked me up with ordinary criminals. The concrete walls dripped with dampness. One small window set high up on the wall allowed in a ray of light. I shared this luxurious accommodation with three middle-aged men and two youths. We had a single straw mattress, barely long enough for all of us to use as a pillow. We lay down on the moist concrete, so cramped for space that all six of us had to turn over at the same time. Nobody could sleep, as the lice began to crawl over us when darkness fell.

I have always prided myself on being able to sleep through anything, but I confess that I did not sleep well or for very long in Pawiak Prison. I could not help feeling anguish as I heard the cries of those beaten and tortured, the shots of the execution squad, and the agonized moans of the dying. Reveille at six a.m. meant everyone had to stand at attention. As I was the only one in my cell who spoke even rudimentary German, I had to stand at attention in our doorway early each morning to report to the guards, "All present".

Breakfast was pitiful. We each received one slice of dry dark bread and half a cup of bitter, black *ersatz* (fake) coffee. After breakfast, everyone listened anxiously from behind the door while the guard read the list of those being taken back to Szucha Avenue that day for cross-questioning by the Gestapo. We all wanted to get out of Pawiak as soon as possible but dreaded what might be done to us at "Szucha", as everyone called the Gestapo headquarters torture chambers. I felt lost and terrified.

For lunch they brought us a cup of wormy cabbage or beet soup, and in the evening we again feasted on one slice of bread and coffee. Before long we came down with violent gastrointestinal upsets that were so bad we couldn't even eat the bread or drink. They allowed us only two trips a day to the little "cowshed" (outhouse) at the end of our corridor, and then only for a few minutes at a time. We were forced to turn a corner of our cell into a latrine. It was disgusting how we lived with lice and human waste, but at least we were still alive. Each of us added our names to the many inscriptions on the wall of our cell. I kept telling myself silently to grin and bear it, but it was not easy. Later I learned that Father and Uncle Norbert had been together in this cell or a nearby one just like it back in 1940.

After a week that felt like eternity in Pawiak, I heard the warder read out my name on the list of those going to Szucha. They took me upstairs to a waiting room and ordered me to stand facing the wall. I turned my head and spotted Stefa standing in a group of women on the opposite side of the room. I turned again to see her better and was beaten for it by a Gestapo man. Stefa cried out in protest, and they shouted at her. I hated being so completely helpless. On the way to Szucha in the Black Maria police van, Stefa and I spoke in whispers to be sure that we would give similar answers to the questions we might be asked. Apparently the Gestapo were arresting more people than they could watch closely, for no guard sat with us. When Stefa and I said goodbye, I felt it was for the last time.

Once inside the Gestapo headquarters, no one was allowed to move or speak. We could hear thuds and screams as we waited in an infamous room known as "the clinic" or "the streetcar" because people sat in a long line of chairs. By the time the officer called me, I was ravenously hungry from the odors of food the Germans were cooking. Whether they intended the smell as a subtle form of torture or not, that's what it felt like.

A Gestapo man asked me what my profession was. I told him I was a student. He ordered me to clean his riding boots, still on his feet. When I had finished, I had to clean the boots of two more Gestapo officers. I seethed with humiliation but hid my feelings.

Then they put me in the "streetcar" until afternoon. I sat facing the blank wall on a one-man bench made of two-by-two planks, small and very uncomfortable. I had to sit still and was not allowed to turn my head. Once, when I did turn it a little, the guard who paced up and down the corridor sneaked up behind me and delivered a blow to my head with his truncheon. I felt the back of my head explode. My forehead dripped with perspiration, and my lips and mouth felt feverish and dry. I was hurting. I was thirsty, and my stomach growled for food. I felt alone and scared.

Interrogation

The same Gestapo man who had arrested me came to get me. I had the shakes by the time I climbed to the second floor and entered the room where other Gestapo men waited. My nerves felt completely out of control. I had to struggle to get hold of myself and not disgrace myself completely in the presence of these thugs.

When they asked if I knew German, I said no, hoping to gain time to think while they translated their questions into Polish. They showed me Ola's false identity papers and asked if I knew her. I told them that the face was familiar, but the name unknown to me. They didn't guess that she had lived with Ludwik's family, and they never found out about her Jewish ancestry. Ola had committed suicide without telling them anything.

Then they showed me a large album of photos and asked if I knew any of the people. They put the album in my hands. I turned the pages and saw the faces of freedom fighters looking out at me, Ola among them. I hoped some of them were free, but I kept turning the pages.

At one page I stopped and said, "I know this one".

"From where?" asked a Gestapo man.

"It is one of my fellow prisoners, and he is in the cell next to mine".

As the Gestapo man's face flushed angry red, I realized how foolish I had been to mock them. When I had looked through the entire album, the Gestapo man changed tactics. He began to speak to me in a fatherly way, trying to get me to believe that he knew everything: If I told him the truth, because of my youth I would be set free. He wanted me to tell him who had brought me into the underground army, and what company I belonged to. I told him that I didn't belong to any secret organization and had never even heard of any such thing. He alternated between threats and pleading.

It was intense and grueling. I kept denying any knowledge of a secret organization. He asked me about Ludwik, because they knew that I lived in his building. I told them that Ludwik was the caretaker of some gardens in Lower Park in Zoliborz near the Citadel and the Vistula River. The park was city property, and many citizens were growing food there. The Gestapo officers studied a map of that area and asked what was the building in the center of the gardens. I was petrified. Struggling to stay calm, I told them it was a shed for storing gardening equipment. They ordered me to take them there. Three Gestapo men armed with machine guns went along in the open Mercedes convertible. They told me that they had orders to kill me if I tried to escape.

We rode through the crowded city by the light of the pale red evening sun. Two roads led to our destination, but I guided the driver by the longer route. Along the way, there was a gate that caused a nice delay. The gate was easily visible from the shed, so that anyone there would have ample warning to get away. I prayed that Ludwik was far away and safe.

As we went down the hill we caught sight of two men running through the potato fields. The POL (Police) on the license plate of the Mercedes had been enough warning for them. After getting through the gate, we accelerated down the hill, screeching to a halt next to the shed. Two of the Gestapo men leaped out and went to check the identity papers of a group of people standing nearby. They detained one young man on leave from labor in Germany. Then they searched the shed. They came back, saying *"Nichts"*. (Nothing.) I was overjoyed and struggled to keep it from showing on my face. When Ludwik heard of my arrest, he must have had the foresight to move our company's car, a stolen German Army Opel, as well as the arms cache hidden in the shed.

The Gestapo took the arrested slave laborer and me back to Pawiak Prison. They told me they would check my story. If I had told the truth, I would be set free. So ended a day on which my whole future depended.

What Next? Auschwitz?

Days passed, infinitely slowly. Incarceration made me feel depressed, weak, and despondent. Then on Sunday, the fourth morning after the ride to Ludwik's shed, I heard my name read on the list of prisoners to be transported to Auschwitz on Tuesday or Wednesday. I knew that I was about to experience for myself what Uncle Norbert had gone through. Anything other than the Szucha Avenue torture chambers seemed preferable.

On Tuesday morning I sat in my cell, totally sunk in despair, thinking that I would probably never see my parents again. As a rule at Pawiak Prison the innocent were sent to Auschwitz, and the guilty were put in front of a firing squad. Being released was almost unheard of. The "capo," the criminal trusty, called to me suddenly, "You are being set free!"

He gave me my release card, and still I could not believe it.

Half an hour later, I sat in the prison's Black Maria on the way back to Szucha Avenue. Three pretty girls sat before me in the van. I started to share my joy with them, but they told me they were to be executed. The Germans had found out they worked for the underground army. They told me their fate simply and openly. The three were sixteen, seventeen, and twenty years old, respectively. I didn't know how to reply. I shook hands with them and promised to say a prayer for them in church. Sometimes, before I go to sleep, I still see all three of them clearly.

At Szucha I sat in a chair in the "streetcar" waiting room yet again. A man near me looked neither human nor animal: His jaw and cheekbones were out of place, covered in dried blood, and his right eye socket was empty, a raw wound. A woman, whose arms were crossed over bloody bandages where her breasts had been, whispered that they had told her she would be put on the rack the next day, and she hoped that everything would end at last. These people were suffering torture and death so bravely for their country or their faith. I wondered if I would be so brave if it happened to me. It was hard to believe that this nice building had been the Ministry of Education before the Gestapo had taken it over. What an education they were giving us prisoners!

That afternoon I was taken to the officer in charge of Szucha Avenue, Major Ludwig Hahn. He was a huge *ubermensch* (elite man) in a dark gleaming SS officer's uniform with silver trim and epaulets. He looked formidable sitting under a huge painting of Hitler. The death's head insignia on his uniform seemed appropriate and fitting.

With my shaven head, dirty clothes, and body shaking with hunger and fatigue, I felt less than human.

To my complete surprise, I noticed two other men at the enormous desk — my father and his aide and translator, Dr. Emil Kipa! It was awful not being allowed to greet my father. Father looked pale and could barely stand. My imprisonment — and the way I looked — must have shaken him to the roots.

Some formalities and a lecture from Major Hahn followed. He told my father that he did not want to set me free because he did not believe that I was innocent. He was only doing so this time because of my age. The next time, he threatened with a glint of steel in his eye, not even the devil himself would be able to help me.

After that, in a dreamlike state, I found myself on the way home. I couldn't believe that I had been set free from Pawiak Prison. I couldn't even talk to my father. All I said was, "Now I know what hell looks like." But whether I said that out loud or to the thousand voices shouting within me, I could not be entirely sure.

I had written the names and addresses of my fellow prisoners all over my underclothes. When I left, I promised that I would contact their anxious families, and I did so as soon as I got home.

Warsaw wasn't safe for me. A couple of days later, I felt I was being shadowed and leaped off a streetcar. A man followed me, leaving no doubt. Uneasy and angry, I threw him off my trail. When I had a chance to tell my father about the incident, he sent me out of the city to my mother's recently purchased country house and farm, called Baniocha. She had sold our house on Felinski Street to get money for our family to survive, and she had used some of the money to buy this farm because it could provide food. The new owners of the Felinski Street house allowed us to remain living there as well. Baniocha was an old estate near Warsaw with about 10 acres of farmland. It was another world entirely, all but untouched by the war. The quiet and calm seemed as unreal as the time I spent in prison, but even in the countryside Poles were being killed.

Ludwik showed up one morning at the gate of Baniocha. I noticed that, for the first time, he seemed depressed. He was preoccupied and worried, and all he wanted to talk about was Stefa. I gave him a detailed report of my imprisonment, and he said, "Well done." The closest he came to a smile was when I described my visit with the Gestapo to the shed in the gardens of Lower Park. He pressed me to give him all the details I could about Stefa, which I did, but he said little in response. Ludwik stayed in hiding with us for a week, then returned to Warsaw. He knew the risk he was taking, as I told him that he was definitely suspected by the Gestapo of being a leader of the *Polnische Banditen* (Polish Bandits).

I spent the rest of the summer in the country with my mother and Wanda in the tranquil countryside. Wanda filled her time with reading, wishing she could go to school. I didn't realize then how much Wanda suffered physically from the meager diet we had during the war. In later life, she had problems with weakened bones and lost her eyesight because of this period of malnutrition. Being older, I had a stronger body when the war began. Mother didn't push Wanda to help with the farm chores because the girl was too weak.

When autumn came, I tried to get into the spirit of the harvest festival, but I felt an intense restlessness. Finally, I decided I had to return to Warsaw.

Collecting Weapons

As soon as I could, I went to see my friend David in Warsaw. I could no longer serve in Eagle Company, and he was not a member of any underground unit either. We decided to do what we could on our own, although it was against the underground army's rules for anyone to act without orders. To do our part to free Poland, we decided we had to get more weapons. There was only one way to accomplish this — disarm Germans, no small feat. It would be crazy to carry out such a plan without a means of defending ourselves, so we first had to find weapons for ourselves. It took almost two weeks, but finally David had a Walther, the small automatic pistol made by the Germans, and I had a large-caliber Smith & Wesson revolver.

Armed at last, we made our way one morning to the forest near the Bielany Airfield, held by the Germans. We decided to hide and wait for a lone soldier. Germans passed in groups of two and three, but never alone. We waited hours, trying to stay keyed up and ready for action. Finally, a lone elderly German on a bicycle came our way. We leaped out. He had no weapons, but we did. The old man pleaded with us to take whatever he had, but please to let him live. David leaped on his bicycle and took off. I made the German lie down in the ravine and kept him there at least 15 minutes to scare him and give us time to escape. Then I made my getaway. In no time at all, I was on the streetcar on my way home.

We made several more attempts to disarm a lone German — with as little success as with our elderly bicycle rider. We followed one man with a briefcase as he got off a streetcar and walked into a dark side street at the edge of the Zoliborz neighborhood near the Opel automobile assembly plant. We didn't get any weapons from him, only a couple of sandwiches, which we devoured, and his wallet and a ring. We let him run for his life, and he made straight for the Opel plant. When we examined his briefcase, we learned that he worked there as a foreman.

David and I were feeling frustrated and impatient. We wandered around the rest of the night, staying under cover until curfew lifted at dawn. We took the first streetcar into the city. It entered Bonifraterska Street by the ruins of the Jewish Ghetto. The remains of the wall were on our right, and German SS policemen guarded the area. Beyond the ruins of the wall, I could see tall, burned-out buildings. In one, a charred skeleton hung in the window frame. It provided a strange comfort that the Ghetto was still there.

David and I left the streetcar in the middle of Krasinski Square and walked around the city. We saw a couple of workers putting a barricade around a manhole.

A German patrol with guns at the ready, slung low toward the pavement, walked past us, and a few civilians crossed the square on their way to work. Now and then a military truck lumbered by.

We were tired, hungry, and exasperated when we noticed a tall German sergeant in full combat uniform, loaded with knapsacks, getting on a streetcar headed to Zoliborz. At his side hung a beautiful pistol, a German Parabellum encased in a shining leather holster. The weapon drew us like a magnet, and we followed him on the streetcar. He went to the front compartment. We Poles were considered subhuman and had to ride in the rear of the streetcar.

What we did next was insane, but we felt driven to extremes. In spite of the incredible danger, we got off at the same stop as our soldier with the lovely automatic — the Warsaw-Gdansk Railroad Station stop, where a viaduct over the trains connected Zoliborz with Bonifraterska Street. Three other German soldiers were getting off there, too, but they seemed in no hurry. We managed to get ahead of that lone soldier in the railroad tunnel under the viaduct. What we had planned would take only a few minutes. We waited until he was about six feet from us and gave him the usual warning, "Arms up or we will shoot!"

The soldier was a seasoned veteran and he reached for his gun. It was kill or be killed! David shot a moment before I did. The soldier fell on his face, probably dead. The roar of the shots still rang in our ears when the other three German soldiers ran out of the stairwell towards us. There was no time to take the pistol from the body of the sergeant. We had to save ourselves. But how? On one side of us were three soldiers with rifles, and at the base of the viaduct along the wall of the Ghetto were German SS guards with machine guns. In the middle was the dead German soldier with the coveted pistol, and we had to escape somehow.

We were lucky. A crowd of people frightened by the sound of gunfire began to run toward the station platform, and the Germans, thinking we were in the crowd, tried to stop everyone by firing over their heads. We made a run for it along the base of the viaduct embankment. Halfway along the grassy slope, we heard rifle bullets whiz past us. We turned, ran over the viaduct away from Zoliborz and down the embankment on the other side. Then we crossed the open area of the street leading away from the Ghetto guards and found refuge in the park behind Bonifraterska Street. From there, after we caught our breath, we made our way to the Old City and merged with the crowds on Market Square.

We were safe, amazingly enough, but our adrenaline was pumping. We went into a small bar for vodka — anything that would steady our nerves. We ended up buying a bottle of mead, an even stronger drink that nearly took our legs out from under us. It did restore us somewhat, even though after drinking it we couldn't have run if our lives had depended on it!

We had gone through hell for that gun, but we had made absolutely no progress in our mission to collect weapons for our company. We ended up empty-handed. I don't think I thought about anything except getting armed.

After we finished our drinks, we returned home via a circuitous and lengthy route to cover our tracks. On the way back, people told us that we had better not go near the Warsaw-Gdansk Railroad Station, where the Gestapo and German SS police were stopping streetcars, searching and arresting all passersby.

The next day the SS police brought a group of twenty perfectly innocent civilians, including old people and children, into the gardens near the station. They tied and gagged these poor souls, and a firing squad executed them. Feeling responsibility for the deaths of these innocents put me into a terribly depressed mood, and people around Zoliborz began to regard me with suspicion. My father sent me to the countryside again, hoping the Germans and the neighbors would forget about me.

Ludwik

I spent a few weeks with my mother at Baniocha but became so restless that I decided again to return to Warsaw. There was only one person I dared to contact: Ludwik.

I visited him. He was living in a different place under a new alias, but with Stefa in prison he had lost his incredible energy and spirit. People tried to convince him to leave Warsaw and join the Home Army's partisans (guerrilla forces hiding in the forests).

The Gestapo knew all about him and were likely to catch up with him at any time. Ludwik chose to stay and fight.

The year 1943 was disastrous for the underground army in Warsaw. Its heroic commander in chief, General "Grot" Rowecki, was among those captured by the Gestapo. The Germans were searching for a lot of specific underground soldiers. I wasn't the only marked man who wanted to do his patriotic duty, and, like many others, I wanted to join the partisans in the forests or the commandos in the city. The partisans ambushed German patrols in the woods and blew up trains in the countryside. The commandos blew up trains in cities and executed Polish traitors. Commandos were actually killing Germans in Warsaw instead of waiting for an uprising like the rest of the Home Army.

Some of Ludwik's other recruits in BASZTA battalion were leaving the city to join the partisans. I think it added to Ludwik's distress that his comrades were leaving his unit to become partisans. I was disappointed to learn that the commandos, after the terrors of the summer of 1943, had temporarily stopped recruiting. I studied the signals instruction manual Ludwik had given me, and in November I was allowed to take over a signals section in Ludwik's Eagle Company.

I was attempting to train six young soldiers in my section when someone came and told me that a few blocks away a man called Ludwik Berger had been shot. Like a fool, I raced to the spot immediately. After a brief search I found — to my horror — bits of flesh, dried blood, and pieces of bone at the foot of the chain-link fence that separated two gardens.

Ludwik Berger — *Goliat, Michal* — my leader. Dead? I would not, could not, believe it.

Standing at attention, I said a prayer and swore an oath of revenge on whoever might have murdered my beloved commander. I stood there for a long time, unable to move. Then I began knocking on doors of nearby houses, asking for details, any information about the incident.

I learned that a few hours earlier the Germans had carried out their daily street search. Large numbers of SS police stopped the streetcars and surrounded them, then ordered all the passengers out and began checking their identity cards. Unfortunately, Ludwik and a friend were in one of the cars. When they saw the SS, they jumped out and ran across the square and down the avenue. Spotting the two men escaping, the Germans opened fire with machine guns and wounded Ludwik in the arm. The two men saw more SS police and ran into a garden. Bleeding badly from his wounds, Ludwik wasted precious time knocking at a door to ask for shelter, but the SS police were too close behind.

Ludwik tried to escape across the gardens. His friend *Lenin* ran the opposite way and managed to escape. A young SS man spotted Ludwik, ran after him, and opened fire with his machine gun. Ludwik found himself at the chain-link fence and started to climb it. The SS man, having used up all his ammunition, threw down his gun and attacked Ludwik with his bare hands. In size they were pretty evenly matched, but the wounded Ludwik could use only one arm and was weakened by loss of blood. He pinned the enemy and sank his teeth into the SS man's throat, but another German arrived and shot Ludwik in the head, blowing out his brains.

Special Forces Commando

After my experiences at the hands of the Gestapo and the death of my beloved Ludwik, I felt such hatred for the Germans that all I wanted was revenge. It was insane, perhaps, considering how terrified I had been during my stay in Pawiak Prison, but I think when Ludwik was killed I went beyond any personal fears. Of course, the whole situation was still terrifying, but many braver men than I admitted to being gripped by fear before rushing into battle. I made a conscious choice, like so many others, to die fighting for freedom.

So I joined a special-forces unit, similar to the U.S. Army Rangers, that was actively involved in fighting. While other underground groups were preparing for the uprising, this crack unit was out killing Germans, derailing trains, sabotaging whatever and wherever it could. I intended to avenge all my friends: the girls tortured by the Gestapo, Ludwik, Uncle Norbert, Zula, every Jew, every Christian, every Pole.

Without Ludwik to vouch for me, I couldn't stay with BASZTA because I was still a wanted man and sometimes found myself being followed, which could put the entire battalion in jeopardy. I left BASZTA and joined the crack unit Ninth Company Commandos, known as "The Reaper." My friend *Wilk*, leader of one of that unit's commando sections, made it possible. He decided, after he heard my stories about the Ghetto, Pawiak Prison and Szucha Avenue, Ola, and Ludwik, that I had won the right to a place in their ranks.

On Christmas Eve, 1943, I attended the first meeting and got to know some of the other commandos: *Slawek*, *Bogdan*, and *Kasper*. For my own new code name, I chose Ludwik's original pseudonym, *Goliat*. Armed with his name and the memory of his dedication to freedom, eventually I was to fight with this unit of commandos during the Warsaw Uprising.

In February 1944 several things happened to fire up our desire to fight the Germans openly. One day I saw a crowd of people gazing at something above the Ghetto wall. As I got closer, I could see for myself: From the upper-story balconies of what had been an apartment house in the Ghetto hung the bodies of 22 of our freedom fighters. The sight horrified me and made my blood run hot with rage. By then, public executions were being held on crowded downtown streets every few days. The Germans didn't realize that such actions only encouraged us to fight back even harder.

Less than two weeks later, we lost a member of our company when his pistol refused to fire during a mission to disarm some Germans in downtown Warsaw.

The occupants of a German military car passing by noticed this confrontation and spotted *Kasper* with the gun in his hand. Moments later, our comrade found himself on his way to Szucha Avenue. We feared the worst and heard nothing about him for some time.

With *Kasper* gone, only six of us remained with *Wilk* (Wolf). That code name suited this determined, no-nonsense commando. He was serious, honest and brave. The men believed in him and trusted him. Only two years older than I, *Wilk* had lied about his age, as I had, to join the commandos. *Wilk*, *Bogdan*, and *Slawek* had all been members of underground Boy Scouts units, known as the Gray Ranks because their pre-war Boy Scout uniforms had been gray. While I had spent my early career in the Eagle Company of the Home Army's BASZTA Battalion, the Gray Ranks were engaging in small sabotage and intelligence operations — good preparation for commando missions.

At the end of February the disturbing news came through that *Wilk* had left for the secret Cadet-Officers School, a training program of the Home Army. Our new leader, *Korwin*, did not seem to like me. Since I was his subordinate, there was little I could do. He had an indecisive air about him, and his acts seemed arbitrary. He also seemed to need to make himself look better by running down others. Yet he was very creative, full of imagination, and had a keen sense of humor.

On March 3, 1944, I turned 15, making me eligible for forced labor or deportation to Germany. It became imperative that I find the best possible legal cover to continue my underground work. I needed an official job that would take the minimum amount of time and allow me to move freely on the streets of the city.

I knew that the Germans respected external signs of officialdom and legality — stamps, documents, signatures and, above all, uniforms. There weren't too many uniforms a Pole could wear and command respect, and so I decided to apply to become a fireman. The city's fire department had performed gallantly during the 1939 Battle of Warsaw and managed to maintain its professional integrity throughout the occupation. I knew that I met all the physical requirements of a volunteer fireman recruit.

On March 20, I was accepted in the fire brigade as a cadet officer. That made four of us in the Ninth Company Commandos who moved about the city freely as firemen. The uniform provided cover for our clandestine activities after curfew. Plus, I was pleased to be able to do such a worthwhile job. I was assigned to the Zoliborz Fire Station in my home neighborhood. We had a large, modern building and a new hook-and-ladder truck that the men maintained beautifully. My job was to be a fire spotter, to alert the firemen to emergencies as early as possible.

Underground Army Commandos
Julian Kulski's Chain of Command
(Pseudonyms are given first, in italics.)

Commander of *Zywiciel* (Life Force) Army Group of
Zoliborz and Kampinos Region:
*Colonel Zywiciel (*M. Niedzielski)

|

Commander of 9th Company, *Zniwiarz* (the Reaper):
Captain Szeliga (M. Morawski)

|

Deputy Commander of 9th Company, *Zniwiarz* (the Reaper)
1st Lieutenant Szymura (G. Budzynski)

|

Commander of Platoon 226:	Replacement Commander of Platoon 226:
‡*1st Lieutenant Szajer* (B. Kunert)	*Cadet-Officer Tadeusz** (T. Huskowski)

Detachment Commander:
Cadet-Officer Korwin (K. Welonski)

|

Detachment Deputy Commander:
Corporal Wilk* (J. Domaniewski)

|

Private Bogdan* (Jan Migdalski)	*Private Krzysztof** (J. Prazmo)
‡*Private Chudy* (*Z. Grubowski)	‡*Private Lewko** (K. Lewandowski)
Private Cygan* (J. Wasowski)	*Private Longinus** (J. Wasowski)
‡*Private Dzani* (J. Lapinski)	*Private Nick* (L. Droszcz)
*Private Gazda (*J. Malinowski)	*Private Sas* (*W. Furmanczyk)
Private Goliat* (**Julian Kulski**)	*Private Slawek* (B. Dziurzynski)
‡*Private Gryf II** (R. Pytlasinski)	‡*Private Thur** (J. Kicinski)
Private Horodynski (Z. Sawicki)	*Private Wrobel* (*Z. Siatkowski)

‡ Killed in Action

* Pseudonym can be translated into English: *Bogdan* (Godgiven), *Chudy* (Skinny), *Cygan* (Gypsy), *Goliat* (Goliath), *Gryf* (Griffin), *Krzysztof* (Christopher), *Lewko* (Lion), *Longinus* (Tall Man), *Sas* (Saxon), *Tadeusz* (Thadeus), *Wilk* (Wolf), *Wrobel* (Sparrow).

Underground Army Commandos (author, top left).

My duty post was on Polish Army Avenue, since I lived near there. My fire-brigade teammate and fellow commando *Bratek* was intelligent, good humored, and about three years older than I. All night long we would indulge in great discussions, enjoying the dual nature of our work. One night we heard Soviet bombers over the city. Powerful German antiaircraft searchlights probed the darkness rhythmically looking for their enemy. We could see the silhouetted shapes of the bombers as they struggled to evade the bright beams and then dropped their incendiaries and other bombs in a frightening and deafening climax. In seeming defiance of the blackout imposed by the Germans, fires broke out in various parts of Warsaw, and we worked hard reporting them to the firefighters so they could bring in fire trucks and other equipment.

Bratek and I became good friends on the fire watch. We talked mostly about our work in the commandos and our common dream — an open fight against the Germans. We knew what we faced and what we had to do. We trained hard. We didn't like having to wait for the uprising to begin.

A Hymn for Poland

On May 3, 1944, I felt an overwhelming urge to do something special to honor Poland's national holiday. The Germans, anticipating demonstrations or armed revolt on that day, had posted three times the usual number of police patrols on the streets, filling trucks with SS police and installing machine guns on every German military building. It enraged me that the Germans had already made it illegal — punishable by death — to sing patriotic hymns in church or to give sermons of a political nature.

I decided to attend the afternoon service at Saint Stanislaw Kostka Church in Zoliborz. Shafts of mellow sunlight reached through its tall, narrow windows to the worshippers below. The sheltered archways were banked with red and white flowers, and soft candlelight cast flickering shadows on the white walls. The church was packed, and I went straight up to the top gallery, also filled with people, and stood by the door leading to the organ loft. I thought it would be grand to hear one of Poland's oldest melodies played during the service.

A crazy, defiant desire spurred me on. Although my pistol was not loaded, I showed it furtively to the violinist who answered the door. He let me in immediately. Thus armed, I walked past a vocalist waiting to sing and approached the organist. I asked him to play the hymn "God, Who Hath Poland Saved." This had been our national hymn since the Uprising of 1830. Neither pistol nor words moved the organist, who kept playing purely religious music while he explained that if he complied, he and his family and the priest would be executed.

I explained to the organist that he would have witnesses — the violinist and the vocalist — to the fact that he had been forced to play the hymn at gunpoint. To my delight, he then struck the chords of our national hymn and, to everyone's surprise and joy, we heard the opening stanzas of the melody that touched the heart of every Pole. Nobody moved. Everyone was stunned. The people in the gallery were the first to begin singing. Soon, the church reverberated with the melody and words of the hymn.

God, who held Poland for so many ages
In Your protection, glory, and great power,
Who gave Your wisdom to her bards and sages
And gave Your own shield as her rightful dower,
Before Your altars, we, in supplication
Kneeling, implore You: Free our land and nation.
Bring back to Poland ancient mights and splendor,
And fruitful blessings bring to fields and meadows.
Be once again our Father, just, tender.
Deliver us from our dire shadows.

As the chorus repeated the refrain, the church filled with the heart-rending plea: "Before Your altars, we, in supplication kneeling, implore You: Free our land and nation."

I didn't wait any longer. With the last emotional words of the hymn resounding in my ears, I vanished into the twilight. The people realized, of course, what might happen to them. Within five minutes, everyone had left the church.

News of that church service spread throughout Zoliborz the next day and cheered people immensely. When I ran into the organist on the street, he bowed politely and smiled at me. I knew he wouldn't betray me. Sometimes the greatest acts of rebellion take place in people's hearts and souls.

The Allies Are Coming!

On June 6, news of the Allied invasion of Europe spread through Warsaw. Forces of Britain, the United States, Canada, and other Allies had crossed the English Channel and had gained a foothold in France. My father thought the

The Allies Are Coming.

invasion might signify a major turning point in the war. He said that many people in City Hall were convinced that liberation of Poland was just around the corner, but he viewed the whole situation with caution. Father thought that things would get a lot worse and reminded us of the Germans' vow to leave no one alive and no buildings standing if they were ever forced to leave Poland.

Adding to the general state of uncertainty and fear in our country, the Soviet Union's Red Army re-entered Poland on July 1, 1944. Day and night, the ground trembled with the roar of guns, always coming nearer. At night, Soviet bombers mounted more raids on our city. The Soviet Union was officially one of the Allied countries, on the side of Britain and the U.S., but Poland's long history of struggle against Russian aggression made us question whether they were trying to liberate us from Germany. We listened to a Polish government-in-exile radio broadcast from England, and I thought perhaps our Prime Minister Mikolajczyk spoke the truth when he said we would have preferred to meet the Soviet Army as allies.

A few days later we heard that leaders of the Polish Communist underground movement had been in Moscow since March and that Stalin was going to make them the future government of Poland. Stalin also promised to provide weapons for the uprising — but only to the Polish Communist People's Army (AL). Our Home Army (AK) was a thorn in Stalin's side just as it had been to Hitler.

Our commander in chief, General Bor-Komorowski, issued a report to all Home Army units stating that the Russians did not recognize the legal government of Poland and were intending to overthrow it. "We must be prepared for an open collision between Poland and the Soviets, and for our part we must fully demonstrate in such a collision the independent position of Poland." We heard that the Soviets intended to incorporate our Home Army units into their puppet Polish People's Army. For this reason, our leaders called off the nationwide uprising that had been set for this month.

The delay allowed us to acquire more weapons. British Royal Air Force airdrops proved a blessing, and we ended up with a few British-made PIAT anti-tank bazookas and brand new Colt 45s. Our company of commandos completed training, and we were not allowed to leave the city just in case W-Day (Warsaw Uprising Day) arrived. I recall being afraid that the Germans would leave Poland without being punished for Ludwik, Ola, Zula, Uncle Norbert, and the millions of others.

I went to visit Marysia, my girlfriend at the time. She was a beautiful blue-eyed blonde, and she looked on me as her knight in shining armor who would take her away from the German horrors. We used to go dancing and have fun with her best friends, Danuta and Barbara, the twins.

That day, however, Marysia was very unhappy with her mother. We went up on the roof of her apartment building for some fresh air — and spectacular views of Zoliborz. I put my arm around her and tried to console her. After a while she calmed down, and while we walked around the roof, I saw an abandoned tank on the Mickiewicz Street side. I asked Marysia if she knew what it was doing there. I hadn't seen a tank on the streets of Warsaw since the Ghetto Uprising in 1943. She said it was broken down, but everybody was afraid to investigate it. Just the month before, the Germans had shot a small boy for touching a motorcycle.

We went for a walk through Zeromski Park and to the top of the viaduct at the Warsaw-Gdansk Railroad Station. There wasn't much activity other than a long line of horse-drawn carts and tired Hungarian Army troops withdrawing from the Russian front. The horses could hardly pull their loads up the viaduct, and alongside them walked a few Hungarian soldiers with machine guns suspended sloppily from their shoulders. Each of them gave us a pitiful but friendly smile and a wave of the hand. I returned the greetings, jealously eyeing the beautiful German weapons going to such complete waste.

I whispered in Marysia's ear, "I wish I had a pint of vodka on me. I've heard you can easily get pistols from these guys in return for vodka."

When we got back to the Glass House, as Marysia's apartment building was called, we had sandwiches and hot tea, but we didn't talk much. A messenger with instructions from *Wilk* came looking for me; I said goodbye to Marysia and returned to headquarters as quickly as I could. *Wilk* had completed his cadet-officer training and had returned to our company. He told me that a state of emergency now existed and, because the commandos lacked accommodations, our entire group would have to stay at my house on Felinski Street.

Our detachment settled in, taking over the whole house. We were not allowed to leave the house at all, not even to go into the garden. My bedroom became our headquarters, and we spent our time making plans. We also spent an inordinate amount of time cleaning our few handguns.

Around July 21, a rumor made the rounds that there had been an attempt on Hitler's life. *Wilk*, thinking Hitler was dead, wanted the uprising to commence immediately. He believed that once we started fighting, the British and Polish air units would drop paratroopers and together we would liberate Warsaw before the Russians arrived. We went on active alert.

Part V

The 1944 Warsaw Uprising

The Eagle Rises

Time dragged while we waited for the moment when the great white eagle of Poland would rise against the enemy. Hundreds of underground soldiers were staying at various houses in Zoliborz. We were going to fight in this part of Warsaw because we were the only commando company in that part of the city. I was lucky to be assigned to Zoliborz instead of to one of the commando units in other parts of the city. I was happy to defend and free my own neighborhood.

All our detachments were busy. Some were engaged in gathering a strange assortment of uniforms — helmets borrowed from the crosses over the graves of Polish soldiers who fell in the 1939 defense of the city, combat camouflage jackets of the SS *Panzer* (tank) units taken from a nearby factory, and whatever else we could find. The girls of our company made red-and-white armbands, the only standard part of our otherwise crazy mixture of civilian and military outfits of all ages, sizes, and colors. The armbands were intended to help us identify each other so we wouldn't mistakenly shoot our own soldiers.

Wilk was the only one dressed in a regular army uniform. I had no idea where he found it. He cut an imposing figure in his gray-green outfit, army boots, field cap with a large white eagle, and Cadet officer's stripe. His Sten gun, a British machine pistol suspended on a leather strap from his shoulder, completed the picture.

During the night the Soviet Air Force bombed Warsaw heavily. On July 30, long lines of heavy tanks from the SS Hermann Goering *Panzer* Division passed along Jerusalem Avenue on the way to Praga, the Warsaw suburb where I used to ride the llama in the zoo, across the Vistula River from the Old City. We heard later that the Red Army had withdrawn under the onslaught of these German reinforcements.

Word came down our chain of command setting W-Hour for 17:00 (5 p.m.) August 1, 1944. Our time had finally come! August 1st was to be our D-Day. The white eagle was ready to strike its prey.

At dawn that day we got the order to move. Our whole platoon gathered at a house on Tucholska Street, just off Zoliborz's main boulevard, Krasinski Street. Additional arms were distributed among us. Around midday, a few of us were chosen to go on patrol to Suzina Street, with our pistols and Sten guns hidden under our capes. We would protect an advance group of our company while they moved arms from one of our hideouts. We received orders not to shoot unless first fired upon.

At the intersection of Krasinski and Suzina Streets, we divided into pairs and waited. I was posted as a lookout on Krasinski. We were hyper-alert to what was happening around us, and we didn't have to wait very long.

Just as the advance group was carrying large packages across Krasinski Street, a German patrol truck turned in and began to drive slowly down the street. Seeing our little column, the Germans brought their vehicle to a screeching halt and opened fire on the men in the middle of the boulevard. Our patrol returned fire from the other side of Krasinski Street. The Germans, surprised by our barrage of gunfire on their flank, turned around to look. That gave the advance group the opportunity to withdraw to Kochowska Street.

We were unaware that this unexpected attack on our handful of men three hours before 5 p.m. would be the premature beginning of the historic 1944 Warsaw Uprising.

The fighting was fierce, and bullets whined over our heads. *Wilk* wounded a couple of Germans with his Sten gun, and they withdrew quickly. *Wilk* took his men to the Lower Park. During the few minutes pause, we opened the packages of arms and distributed the guns, hand grenades, and ammunition. I drew an old Polish army rifle — the Warszawiak 1937 — with ammunition. Then we took up new positions in buildings along Krasinski Street.

It was then early afternoon. Two huge German trucks, loaded with special SS anti-insurgency commandos, stopped on the boulevard and began firing into Suzina Street with machine guns and rifles, and we opened up on them. Their bullets roared over our heads, hitting the walls of the apartment building from which we fought. This exchange of fire gave me my first opportunity to use my newly acquired rifle. After half an hour's engagement, two of our men had been wounded and were being carried to a nearby house.

The Germans hadn't really been able to reach us with their fire, so they sent a sharpshooter to the end of the street opposite us in order to gauge our exact location. He showed great bravery, as his mission pretty well marked him for certain death. To our amazement, the sharpshooter, without any cover, advanced with stops and starts to cover the distance from the Germans trucks to our end of the street. As he faced us, a bullet fired by Cadet Officer *Mirski* dropped him. The Germans withdrew their trucks, and we fled to a house on Mieroslawski Street, where we intended to stay until it was time to rejoin our company.

At exactly five o'clock, as originally planned, a wave of explosions and bursts of automatic rifle fire set off the uprising throughout the whole city. In the middle of the dust and fire, red-and-white flags — not seen since 1939 — were raised along the streets and fluttered from windows and rooftops to hail this great moment. The white eagle was back!

The Germans stationed tanks on the corners of the main boulevards and squares of Zoliborz, their deadly barrages of shells and machine gunfire preventing our units from crossing the streets. The sounds of the battle — shells bursting, bullets whining, the ack-ack of machine guns — could be heard all over Zoliborz. W-Hour had arrived.

With support from a heavy Tiger tank, the Germans attacked the building on the corner of Krasinski and Suzina Streets, and we decided to move down Krasinski Street to Zeromski Park. When we reached the lower part of Krasinski Street, we saw that it was being swept by tank fire. German machine guns had been placed so low that the bullets cut off the leaves of the potato plants growing in the center strip of the boulevard. But we knew we had to cross. Crouching with my rifle in my hands, I ran at a terrific speed but then was pinned down in the middle of the road. I couldn't move, and in horror I watched the tank train the muzzle of its big gun on my position. The first shell dropped about twenty-five yards from where I lay, and the next one hit even closer.

They were shelling on our left, right, and center. There was no time to think or to hesitate. We all jumped up and in one rush reached the other side of the boulevard. While I had been pinned down in the middle, a bullet had hit my right arm and cut the sleeve, but I had only been grazed. Again, Lady Luck had kissed me. *Bogdan* had been wounded badly in the leg, and we managed to go back and get him. On reaching the cover of the building on the other side of the boulevard, we left our wounded with underground army medics who were on the scene. One of the nurses dressed my arm and gave me some water. We sat in the courtyard waiting for the next skirmish. An old lady, weeping tears of joy that the longed-for uprising had come at last, came over and blessed us with the sign of the cross.

Night fell, the shooting stopped and silence reigned in Zoliborz again. The only sound that disturbed the silence was the crackle of flames from burning houses. Slowly, survivors of the dispersed units regrouped on the streets of Zoliborz and began to advance toward the building on Krasinski Street that served as headquarters for our company.

When we arrived, we heard that during the day there had been heavy losses. Our detachment had been lucky, only one badly wounded — *Bogdan* — and *Wacek* missing in action. Still, every casualty was a major loss for such a small force. Nevertheless, we remained strong in spirit and resolve, even if our numbers, ammunition, and arms didn't match those of the Germans.

The Great Kampinoska Forest

We were so hungry and tired we could hardly stand. After a brief break, the order to march put us on our feet again. Our detachment consisted of our leader, *Korwin*, deputy leader *Wilk*, and 16 other men, including *Thur*, *Longinus*, and me, *Goliat*. We shouldered our weapons and started off around midnight in a gentle drizzle and withdrew stealthily from Zoliborz. The entire capital lay under a rainbow of fire that raged all over the city. We managed to pass the German antiaircraft-gun positions without being seen. Our destination was the Great Kampinoska Forest beyond the German-held airbase at Bielany.

After about an hour's brisk march, we found ourselves near Bielany. By then the rain had turned into a downpour and we were all soaked to the skin. I had appropriated my father's lightweight uniform from the First World War, and I didn't have a sweater or overcoat. The others were as inadequately clothed as I was. Trembling with cold, hunger, and fatigue, shielding my rifle under my thin jacket, I marched along with the others. We hurried to get as far away from the city as possible before daybreak.

Just after passing Bielany, *Baron's* hand grenade accidentally exploded on his belt and opened a gaping wound to his abdomen. It was one of the homemade grenades that so often proved to be unsafe, and fragments of this grenade had also wounded *Akropolites*. *Baron* was dying and begged us to put him out of his agony. He knew that we could not take him with us, but we refused to leave him for the Germans. We were all horrified at the idea of shooting one of our own, but *Baron* pleaded with us to honor his last request.

We were a very downcast group of commandos as we left our dead comrade behind and continued our march to the forest.

By morning gray, wet fog trailed across the fields, hovering over the hillocks and blurring the birches and willows. In the distance we saw a ribbon of woodland. We marched across soggy fields grown high with wild grass, past slumbering hamlets toward the wilderness of the Great Kampinoska Forest, where we hoped to find safety and retrieve weapons from airdrops.

When we reached a small hamlet, we could make out a menacing German spotter plane circling overhead, and Colonel *Zywiciel* gave the order to end the march. Our next orders were to place machine-gun nests around the village and to send a few patrols out to scout the surrounding countryside. Finally, we threw ourselves down in a hayloft.

After a short rest, our village hosts gave us soup with some potatoes, which we gobbled down. However, the soup only whetted our appetites, and we knew we had to have something solid to eat. Many of us were still growing teenaged boys, and we had been operating on adrenaline and short rations for too long. *Longinus* and I decided to search the village for food.

During our search we realized that any hens that had survived the raids of other hungry young soldiers were locked up in huts and well guarded. We passed through the entire village without finding a single hen, but as we reached the end of the street we heard a sound that was like music to our ears — the squealing of a pig. Immediately, we entered the hut and ordered the peasant woman to take us to the animal.

The woman, sensing that her pig was in danger, told us her neighbor had a much bigger pig. We replied that we did not need a big one. She eyed the rifles slung over our arms and opened the gate to reveal a lovely fat pig lying on the straw.

We aimed our rifles and *Longinus* gave a short burst from his Sten gun. The wounded pig was strong and still tried to escape over a wall. I gave it the finishing shot. We knew what the pig meant to the woman, and we paid her 500 zloty and allowed her to cut off the head as food for her children. Then we hung the carcass on a thick pole, put it on our shoulders and headed back to our headquarters. En route we received many jealous looks. Our friends hailed us as conquering heroes and took the pig into our hosts' hut, where some of our group began cooking it on a spit.

During the evening, two teenaged girls who had sneaked through enemy lines brought fresh orders from General Bor-Komorowski. The whistle signaling us that the pig was ready to eat sounded at 11:30 that night. We gathered eagerly, and the roasted pig was cut up and distributed. That was when they informed us that in 15 minutes we would head back to Warsaw! With our hands full of steaming pieces of hot pork and our fingers dripping with tasty fat, gorging ourselves, we started marching.

Battling Back to Zoliborz

We were very tired but started the return march with great excitement. We were going to fight the enemy and defend our homes and families. It was raining again, but the thought that we were returning to Warsaw fortified us.

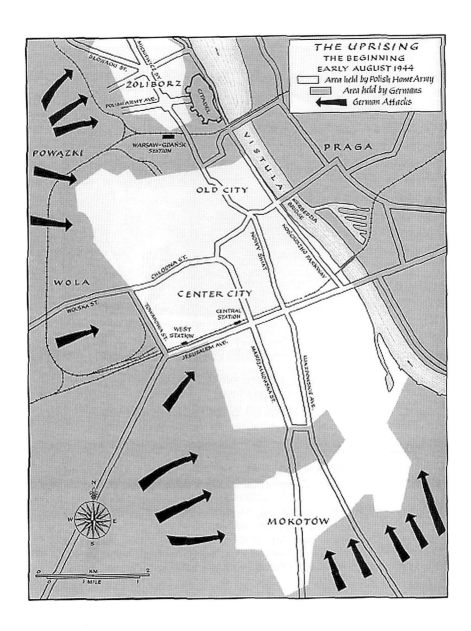

THE UPRISING
THE BEGINNING
EARLY AUGUST 1944

Area held by Polish Home Army
Area held by Germans
German Attacks

ŻOLIBORZ

POWĄZKI

PRAGA

WARSAW-GDAŃSK STATION

CITADEL

SŁOWACKI ST.

MICKIEWICZ ST.

POLISH ARMY AVE.

OLD CITY

V I S T U L A

KIERBEDZIA BRIDGE

NOWY ŚWIAT

KOŚCIUSZKO PARKWAY

CHŁODNA ST.

CENTER CITY

WOLA

WOLSKA ST.

TOWAROWA ST.

WEST STATION

CENTRAL STATION

JERUSALEM AVE.

MARSZAŁKOWSKA ST.

UJAZDOWSKIE AVE.

MOKOTÓW

N
W   E
S

0   KM   2
0   1 MILE   1

We ran into enemy troops just past the little hamlet of Laski, where our column halted. Instead of an exchange of fire, there seemed to be only an exchange of words. Soon, the news passed among the ranks that the "enemy" was a Hungarian infantry unit, and their commanding officer had wanted to speak to our officers.

The exchange took place in German, with marked Polish and Hungarian accents. Only isolated phrases reached my ears in the pitch dark and pouring rain. I heard words about the centuries-long friendship between Hungary and Poland, the longed-for end to the war, and of better times to come. There was no sympathy for the Germans. The dialogue ended with the Hungarians giving us permission to pass unharmed. The officers exchanged salutes, and the column marched again. As we trooped through the puddles, the Hungarians waved, wishing us Godspeed.

The rain increased to a deluge that threatened to separate us. Those responsible for finding the right way often took wrong turns. The column broke, becoming longer and longer. I worried about my rifle, which was getting wet in spite of all my efforts to protect it.

At long last we reached Wawrzyszew, the village closest to Zoliborz, and the rain let up so we could see each other again. I had actually been marching asleep on my feet. I had not believed that was possible until I tripped on a protruding, gnarled tree root and lurched into the man in front of me, which woke me up.

The stillness of the dawn found us in an open field. A group of officers stood against the wooden fence surrounding a homestead, probably discussing what to do with their wet troops. If we were spotted in Wawrzyszew, our column would be destroyed by German artillery in nearby Powazki. In the distance the outlines of the Workers' Conquest Housing Colony, a public housing complex beyond Wawrzyszew near Bielany, emerged through the haze. Situated on a triangle of roads, the housing complex presented the only feasible hiding place.

When we reached the housing complex, we received orders to take up positions in its apartment blocks and surrounding homes. Even though our enemy commanded the Bielany Airfield with antiaircraft artillery, and front-line SS troops held the nearby Central Institute of Physical Education, we were in a good mood. In front of our position was a long field that reached to Zoliborz, and on the left, large apartment houses gave us some protection against the battalions of the SS housed in the Institute. Still, there was serious danger here for all of us. We were ordered not to fire without a direct order from Colonel *Zywiciel*, so as not to disclose our positions prematurely.

At 8 a.m., a German patrol appeared in the open field in front of us. Eight *Luftwaffe* (Air Force) men, carrying machine guns and rifles, walked along slowly talking among themselves, apparently unaware that hundreds of us were hidden nearby. When they were about 110 meters from us, they started to pay more attention and advanced in line formation.

We were frustrated by our order not to fire, but when the Germans were about 35 meters from our location, a shot rang out from a distant house to our left. The Germans began to withdraw, surprised but firing back in the direction from which the shot had come.

Finally, we got our orders to fire, and we opened up immediately on the retreating Germans. Lieutenant *Szajer* and I were firing from the same window. His second shot wounded the patrol leader, who fell to the ground and moaned in agony for an hour until he died.

Now our position had been discovered. After about an hour, more Germans were sent out, more of them than in the first group and with more machine guns. Yet because our first salvo had been light, the enemy had underestimated our strength and sent only about twenty men to take us.

They advanced in a series of haphazard dashes, firing at our windows with their machine guns and rifles. A hail of bullets broke our windows and shattered the tall ceramic-tiled stove in the room. The sofa and carpet caught fire from an incendiary round, but we managed to extinguish the flames. More and more of our troops began to fire on the Germans and after half an hour's time they withdrew and took shelter behind the sandy hillocks in the field.

Our commando company — the only one really armed — was given the job of securing the outposts. The 229th Platoon and the 226th, my platoon, were ordered to take up positions in houses on Zeromski Street. Our section was ordered to a forward position to seize a house there. We examined our Sten guns and rifles carefully and proceeded under the cover of gardens to carry out our task. After leapfrogging across a road under enemy machine-gun fire, we reached the designated house. The frightened inhabitants had already spent the whole morning in the cellar. When they saw us, armed to the teeth, they vacated the premises in double-quick time.

We explored the house. Then *Korwin* placed a few of us at windows on two-hour shifts. Machine-gun volleys and shells exploded constantly. Every five minutes or so, a bullet or fragment of a mortar shell entered the room, hitting the furniture and walls. An unexpected letup gave me time to think while I crouched below the window.

I thought about Ludwik. We were finally doing what he had dreamed of for four long years. We were in the thick of battle against the occupiers, and the man who had brought me into the fight, who had steeped all of us in the need to fight and perhaps to die for freedom, was not there. I hoped he would have been proud and pleased with us.

Feeling very uncomfortable on the hard floor, I turned onto my other side and noticed a photograph of a beautiful girl on the piano. The face seemed familiar to me. After a moment, I realized that it was my cousin, Ania Marjanska, who lived in Komorow, near Warsaw. Then I remembered that her family had a house on this street. It struck me as a strange coincidence to be in her home now.

All hell broke loose that afternoon. Shells from tanks and heavy mortars fell on our commandos still holding positions at the public housing complex. We were now completely cut off from the rest of our company. Occasionally, a Tiger tank passed along the street, so close to the house that it nearly touched the walls. The earth trembled with heavy explosions, and we could hear German voices quite plainly. We were in a hopeless situation, well behind enemy lines. If we were discovered, we would not be able to defend ourselves for more than a few minutes.

Korwin had found a small door in the cellar that led to a tiny cubbyhole under the stairs. After removing all traces of our stay, he ordered us to hide there. The space was tiny, about six feet long and five feet high at most. We sat with each man's head resting against the back of the man in front, knees drawn up to our chins. We hung on to our precious weapons and tried to ignore the growling of our stomachs. Stiff and cramped, we waited while the battle continued in its full fury.

With anguish and frustration, we thought about our friends fighting and dying while we sat under the stairs doing nothing. We decided that if we were attacked, we would fight to the end and then explode our hand grenades — a kinder fate than being captured alive. Every one of us agreed on that point.

At the end of the day, the battle ended, and we heard no more German voices. After six hours of physical contortions, we were finally able to leave our hiding place. During our confinement we had received no orders, so *Korwin* decided that we should return to the public housing complex in the dark and attempt to rejoin our company.

On the way, we saw the complex in flames. Only a few walls and chimneys remained to identify the wreckage as apartment houses. German shells had bored huge holes in the gardens, and we saw the mutilated bodies of our comrades. When we reached our company's survivors, *Korwin* reported to the commander, and our friends gave us a hearty welcome. Then they told us what had happened during the battle, filled us in about the details of their hairraising exploits, and reported who had died or been wounded.

Our units had suffered terrible casualties that day. The poorly built apartment houses of the complex did not protect our soldiers against artillery or tank fire. The deputy company commander, Lieutenant *Szymura*, had received his third serious wound in two days, and yet he commanded his platoon to the very end. Another platoon, the 230th, lost 17 men during a counterattack.

Our detachment was ordered to go onto the battlefield to gather arms and ammunition from the dead. We were not as exhausted as the others, and we were glad to do something useful. We moved quietly among the moonlit sand dunes. Every few feet we saw a body lying grotesquely twisted, often a soldier of our own company. I found one boy lying on his face and removed the rifle that was locked tightly in his grasp. A bullet had passed through his helmet into his forehead. I took his helmet, a priceless possession.

At a distance of three hundred yards from our positions lay Germans, young and old, torn, twisted, and covered with blood. It seemed to me that they were sleeping peacefully for the first time in a long while. The field of death made a deep impression on me. It was the first time I had seen so many fragmented bodies and such horrible gaping wounds. Despite my reactions to these horrors of war, I followed orders and collected helmets, arms, and ammunition.

Shortly after we finished our work on the battlefield, Colonel *Zywiciel* issued orders for us to move toward Zoliborz. We left the wounded in the care of the inhabitants of Bielany and sent soldiers without weapons back to the Great Kampinoska Forest. Starting out at 11 o'clock at night, it took four hours to cover a distance that usually took forty-five minutes. The Germans were sweeping the fields with searchlights and rockets so that every few minutes we had to stop and drop to the ground. We even took off our shoes and tried not to breathe. If the Germans had noticed us in the middle of that field, their heavy artillery would have wiped us out. We were lucky. We passed by the enemy's artillery positions safely. More than 1,200 of us reached Zoliborz. In this way, we regained Zoliborz with the solemn promise to defend it and its inhabitants to the last drop of our blood.

We billeted in apartment houses and finally slept. Civilians tried to look after us. They helped in every way they could with food or clothing. In retrospect, the uprising was astonishing: underground soldiers fighting in the streets of Warsaw, aided and abetted by civilians, united with a passionate zeal to free the city from tyranny and oppression.

Our Flag Flies Over Warsaw Again

On August 4, much of Warsaw was ours again! The red-and-white flag of Poland finally flew all over the scarred but proud city. People tore down the hated swastikas and burned them. A heady feeling overcame us all. Our flag was flying again even though we knew the war was not over.

From early in the morning, civilians worked with the underground army, building barricades and digging anti-tank and communication trenches throughout Zoliborz. They used every available material: overturned streetcars, furniture from nearby houses, garbage cans, even bricks from destroyed buildings. Some of the barricades were so high that they reached the second floors of the adjacent buildings.

The civilians were eager to help, and work on the fortifications proceeded swiftly. The enemy withdrew from Zoliborz. We held a large area, but unfortunately it was strangled by the railroad lines to the south and west, cutting us off from the rest of our army.

Wehrmacht and SS formations were quartered in fortified strongholds all around us. They were too close for comfort. The Germans held the Chemical Institute at the top of Polish Army Avenue. They commanded both sides of the Warsaw-Gdansk railway viaduct to the south. They were in the Citadel and along the banks of the Vistula River in the east, as well as in the old Chemical Warfare School in Marymont in the north, in the public school building on Kolektorska Street, and in the Central Institute of Physical Education in the northwest.

The Germans defended most heavily the area along both sides of the Warsaw-Gdansk railway line. This strategy cut us off from the rest of the liberated parts of the city. From our standpoint, our separation from the group holding the Old City was most unfortunate. The only means of communication between Zoliborz and the Old City was through the underground sewer pipes. The enemy had followed the old dictum "divide and conquer."

We cleaned our weapons and remained in a state of constant alert. While we were stationed in apartment buildings on Suzina Street, new red-and-white armbands stamped with the number of each platoon had been distributed among us. The stamps prevented unauthorized use of the armbands, which were more important than ever for quick identification as so many of us were wearing captured helmets and other parts of German uniforms.

We passed the time talking to the nurses, who listened eagerly to the stories of yesterday's battle. One girl came frequently to our quarters, her arms full of food, as she knew we were very short of rations. Although the girl was lovely, I looked forward to seeing only one person — Marysia. I was delighted when she showed up, although I had no idea how she found out where we were. She looked so beautiful that the mere sight of her brought a glow to my heart.

Soon all the visitors left, and from early afternoon heavy artillery fire fell on our immediate area. Our company received the order to move into the cellars where the inhabitants of the building were already sheltering. While we waited, we started to sing. This previously hidden talent made the waiting easier to endure, and the rest of the company and the occupants of the building listened enraptured. The cellar rang with songs such as "Storm Company," "Little Lieutenant," "A Kiss Is as Sweet as a Date," "Unfaithful Mary," and many other soldiers' songs, including our company anthem, which had been written by *Korwin*.

On Saturday, August 5, two detachments of our platoon received orders to defend the still-unfinished barricade at Slowacki Street. There we repelled three enemy attacks with hand grenades, rifles, Sten guns, and machine guns. Only two of our men were wounded, but the Germans lost eighteen.

While we engaged in this counterattack, the 229th Platoon fought against German troops who were supported by a tank, which had attacked from the river toward Wilson Square. The 230th encountered an enemy patrol on Krasinski Street. We repelled German attacks everywhere, and the day's fighting brought us complete victory.

We weren't far from Felinski Street, and in the evening Aunt Stacha, dust-covered and tired, arrived at our headquarters. Marysia had told her where to find me. Aunt Stacha brought us wine and food. She told me that my father was with the General Staff of the Home Army in Warsaw's Old City, which was under the heaviest fire.

The Germans had attacked the Old City with airplanes, tanks, infantry, and all available artillery, including enormous railway guns. The dreadful pall of smoke over the Old City was visible from Zoliborz, and we could hear the unceasing explosions of bombs and artillery shells. Every hour, enemy Stukas flew over Zoliborz from the Bielany Airfield, dropping bombs. It was outright slaughter: We did not have one antiaircraft gun in the entire city.

We heard that the Germans had organized a brigade from Soviet prisoners of war — Ukrainians and Central Asians lured into fighting by the promise of plunder, food, and vodka. That brigade hit the westernmost suburb of Wola hard, taking no prisoners, killing men and children on sight, and raping women before shooting them. Polish forces took prisoners and kept them alive, but German officers had orders from Hitler himself to shoot all Polish men, women, and children who were captured. The enemy herded hundreds of civilians in front of their tanks as shields, knowing that Polish freedom fighters would not open fire on innocent victims. We knew what had happened in the Ghetto, so we weren't surprised that the Germans were capable of such barbaric acts.

We received our orders to hold the most exposed area of Zoliborz, and my platoon ended up at the front of our own lines, surrounded by the enemy's positions. We occupied my old fire-fighting headquarters on Slowacki Street, and I explained its layout to my comrades. We set up observation posts at several windows, and then slept in the dormitories previously used by the firemen.

For three days we watched covertly as the Germans tried to determine if we were still holding the building. Using heavy artillery, they advanced closer toward the barricade farther down the street. Our platoon had only forty men, yet we watched a couple hundred Germans preparing for the skirmish. They passed our building and attacked the barricade way behind us. Under continuous heavy fire from all sides, they started to retreat slowly, but still we waited. When the order finally arrived, we unleashed a murderous fire that took the Germans entirely by surprise.

They regrouped, just beyond our range, and set up machine guns to deter us from picking up weapons from their fallen comrades in the middle of the boulevard. Even so, we were too poorly armed to miss the opportunity of acquiring more weapons. *Longinus* went after a large submachine gun, and I retrieved an automatic rifle. All told, we captured rifles, ammunition and one light machine gun. I took a pair of boots from one of the bodies, and they fit, so I was able to replace my own tattered shoes.

During the two months of our long-awaited uprising, we saw plenty of battle action and sustained enormous casualties. We remained under steady and heavy artillery fire during the ten days that we held the fire brigade building. We had reports of the action in other parts of the city. We learned that General Erich von dem Bach, the new commander-in-chief of all German units, had been instructed by Hitler not to take prisoners and to eradicate Warsaw from the face of the earth. Now we understood that even if we surrendered, the Germans would shoot us.

We had an unexpected windfall when a German truck drove at breakneck speed towards our building. We let it get very close before stopping it with our fire. Germans leaped out. One was killed, but two got away. The truck remained in the open under continuous crossfire, until Cadet Officer *Zawada* jumped in and tried to drive it away. In his haste, he crashed into the corner of our building and couldn't budge the truck from the spot. We discovered that the truck was filled with wooden crates of hand grenades. Overjoyed at our luck, we unloaded it quickly, aware that the Germans would now press their attack even harder. Just as we put the last crate in the cellar, a relentless artillery shelling began, filling the building with dust and debris and perforating the walls like Swiss cheese.

After ten days of holding the fire brigade building, we were relieved and sent away from the front line for a brief rest. During that long siege, a number of our men had been injured.

I was looking forward to sleeping in a real bed and enjoying edible food for the first time in a month, but strain, exhaustion, and hunger finally caught up with me. I ran a high fever that weakened me so that I could not move. The owners of the apartment building where we billeted looked after me, and my dear Aunt Stacha brought me food and news.

The rest of the city had gone through hell while my company was fighting in Zoliborz. The couriers made perilous trips through the fetid sewers in order to maintain communications with the Old City. Partisan units, newly arrived from eastern Poland, failed to break through the German lines holding the Old City, and one hundred of our soldiers were killed or wounded in the field in front of the Warsaw-Gdansk Railway Station.

The Home Army organized a full-scale joint attack from both sides of the railway and our company attacked the Warsaw-Gdansk station itself. The strategy was to divert the attention of the enemy while the partisans reached the Old City. The night was unseasonably cold, and our summer clothes provided no protection from the damp ground. We tied rags around our boots to muffle the sound of our feet on the pavement during the initial attack.

Huge, blinding flares lit up the field, and long salvos of machine gunfire interrupted the quiet. The German and Ukrainian troops, jittery and trigger-happy, were ready for us.

The order came at 2:00 a.m. to take the hill where the railroad tracks were. As our companies were crossing the avenue, the sky was lit by hundreds of marker flares, and the night turned into day. These red stars hung for a long time, casting an eerie light on our storm troops pinned down in the shadows of the buildings, making us easy targets. Hundreds of shells from automatic weapons and tracer bullets rained down on us, spattering against the walls of apartment houses. In spite of the hurricane of enemy gunfire, in spite of huge shells from an armored train that exploded, making craters and decimating our ranks, we continued to advance up the bare hill. Towards the summit we were pinned down by continuous crossfire. The cries of the wounded rose above the incessant rattling of heavy gunfire, and our combat nurses crossed the road in vain attempts to help. The order to retreat was passed along. The battle was lost. White flares bathed the fields in ghostly light, illuminating dozens of dead and wounded freedom fighters.

Our company sustained heavy losses, and among the dead was the head of our nurse corps. *Mitis* was a middle-aged woman whose husband had died in Auschwitz and whose two sons the Germans had executed. Although wounded herself, she went into the battle to dress the wounds of our fallen soldiers. A dum-dum bullet struck her in the back, killing her. I also lost a close friend, *Gryf*, who died after hours of agony from serious stomach wounds. Towards the end, he became delirious, screaming, "Attack, boys, attack! Avenge my father!"

Escaping through the sewers.

Father Goes Underground, Literally

After the battle I received another visit from Aunt Stacha, who told me how my father had escaped from the Old City through the sewers. With unusual precision, AK (Home Army) officers had organized the evacuation of the survivors of the Old Town — freedom fighters and members of the city administration, still under continuous enemy fire from both ground and air. After a couple of days of anxious waiting, AK officers had assigned my father a place in the group heading through the sewers to Zoliborz.

Members of the group gathered around the manhole in the center of Krasinski Square in the Old City where today stands the monument to the Warsaw Uprising. The young but experienced guide was already there. He explained in an authoritative voice all the dangers awaiting them below. He ordered them to maintain total silence during the passage. The Germans, aware that the insurrectionists were using the sewers, would throw grenades down if they heard the slightest noise.

It was a gorgeous full-moon night. One by one Father and the rest of the group descended into the stinking city sewer, holding tightly to the slippery metal rungs. With the young guide at the head, they formed a line holding on to each other. Slowly and carefully, they started the ghastly journey on the slippery floor of the sewer.

At first, the filthy liquid — full of human excrement and pieces of garbage — reached only to their knees, but as they moved further in total silence and darkness, the water level rose and the speed of the current started to increase.

Father was second in line. As they reached the section of the sewer where the current was strongest, he slipped and fell. Without uttering a sound, he sank to the bottom of the disgusting, stinking liquid. The guide said, "One of ours has drowned." As the strong current carried Father into a side channel, further and farther away from the main sewer channel, he was certain that it was the end.

He told me later that he was unaware of how long he had been carried by the current when suddenly he hit barbed wires dropped into the sewer by the Germans as a barricade. His legs caught on it and tore his flesh. The barbs made deep cuts, causing excruciating pain. However, the current approaching the Vistula River was so powerful that the enemies' barricade failed to stop him. After a certain time, his wounded body reached the main channel again at another juncture with the side channel. At that exact moment his original column, still in total darkness, was passing the exact same juncture and he was able to rejoin them. By a miracle, God had saved him!

The others helped him to his feet and, with their aid, he continued on the ghastly journey. He dreamt of fresh air, daylight, and the end of this underground hell.

The last part of the trip was the hardest as the sewer channel began to climb. For an exhausted, wounded older man, it seemed beyond his strength to continue. Every step seemed an eternity. At the end, when the group emerged from a moonlight-filled manhole exit right in front of the convent of the Sisters of the Resurrection, Father must have felt as though his hopes and very life had somehow been resurrected. The nuns gave him first aid, and he managed to hobble along until he reached our home on Felinski Street. The raw sewage had caused serious infection in his wounds. He was now bedridden at home.

Defending Zoliborz

With the Old City a pile of rubble, Zoliborz remained under constant bombardment. On the last day of August, waves of Stuka dive-bombers flew over our positions and Wilson Square, swooping low over the roofs of the apartment houses. A dreadful explosion shook Zoliborz when bombs hit the enormous modern apartment building called the Glass House on Mickiewicz Street. The front wall of the Glass House had collapsed, exposing all the floors. My heart sank: Marysia lived there! I wanted to run over there immediately to help, but we had to stay put. The order arrived later: "Detachment to dig up the ruins on the double."

I started out first, forgetting military discipline and leaving my detachment behind. The wing of the building where Marysia lived was relatively intact, but the middle section had collapsed into the cellar where the inhabitants sought shelter. Some rescue squads were already at work, and I started digging too. We heard the groans of victims buried under the broken bricks and glass. After an hour we succeeded in digging out a middle-aged woman whose legs were smashed and twisted. She told us that ten other people had been with her before the bombs fell. Then we began to see a head, a leg, or an arm under the debris, signs that we were coming to more bodies. We uncovered a man next, dead and damaged.

After three hours of frantic digging, we found a woman with a baby in her arms. Both were alive, although injured and frightened. When we went to the back of the building for a breather, we found the whole garden full of corpses, mostly women and children. Many of us who had not cried before wept at the terrible sight of that civilian disaster. But I found, among the survivors standing in a dazed huddle, Marysia, miraculously unscathed.

September signaled the fall of the Old City. The sheer numbers of the enemy, their bombers and huge tanks, their endless supply of high-tech weapons made our task seem impossible. Yet the Home Army, in spite of exhaustion and starvation, doggedly waged counterattacks. They used up their last reserves of ammunitions to keep the Germans from entering Krasinski Square where a manhole, which assured freedom, was located. Leaving only token guards on the barricades, platoon after platoon, company after company, formed a long line and with perfect discipline descended into the stinking, swift-flowing sewers. The trip took four hours through waist deep sludge and poisonous fumes. They formed a human chain, each link holding tightly on to the next, snaking underground – slowly, in total darkness and silence.

After taking the Old City, the enemy trebled its attacks on our positions. The Germans wanted to finish us off as soon as possible. They began mass air raids on Zoliborz. About the same time the Red Army captured Praga, the suburb on the other side of the Vistula. Our detachment, along with the entire 229th Platoon, received orders to take over and defend the Opel factory, another forward outpost. The plant covered an extensive area, bordered on the west by the railroad tracks leading from the Warsaw-Gdansk station toward Palmiry and the Great Kampinoska Forest. I remembered the Opel plant well from early years of the occupation. I had spent many nights there with a friend exploring the underground labryinths, searching for weapons and ammunition stored by the Polish Army in September 1939. Ludwik had used it for night meetings and arms caches. David and I had attempted to take arms from the German foreman near this factory wall just a year earlier.

We checked out the entire facility, established observation posts in the tallest buildings, and dug communication trenches under cover of night. We made good use of the reinforced concrete bunkers constructed by the Germans before the onset of the uprising. The Opel factory was very difficult to defend, because of its location next to an open field, about 600 yards from the enemy's guns, tanks, and infantry. About a mile away, German SS units were quartered in the Chemical Institute, and the tanks of a *Waffen SS Panzer* division were parked smack in the middle of our gardens.

Some of our men were assigned to guard the main gate of the compound. They made themselves at home in the adjoining guardhouse. Some Germans knocked at the big gate, not realizing that we now held the Opel factory. We let our "visitors" in and properly welcomed them — with a hail of bullets.

Gazda, *Thur*, and I had orders to hold a roofless building, still under construction, known as the brick kiln. We had three main observation posts there. Someone had to watch the small gate leading into the gardens, as it would be easy for the Germans to reach this place under the cover of the trees. The second observation post, mine, was on the exposed mezzanine floor, accessible only by a long ladder. My post was vital but very dangerous. Any movement noticed there by the enemy would bring in a blast of machine gunfire. The third observer had to watch the gardens from the ground. We took turns at these three points every three hours in order to keep awake, for we were on duty around the clock.

Zoliborz was still under heavy artillery fire, but the Russian antiaircraft guns right across the river inhibited the German Stuka dive-bombers from conducting their missions at will. I spent long nights in this lonely and dangerous place. The need for constant vigilance, combined with cold and hunger, made me weary but fiercely possessive about this pile of bricks that my comrades and I were defending.

After about a week, our position attracted attention, and from my observation post I noticed artillery gun muzzles pointing toward us. I had just enough time to slip down the ladder before exploding shells shook the brick kiln. After each burst, I returned to my post. At midday a Stuka flew close to eliminate me. It came so close that I could see the pilot's expression as he fired directly at me, somehow missing. In that moment the war suddenly became totally personal. The plane then rose in the sky with a thunderous roar and terrifying whistle; it disappeared over the city, leaving an empty ominous silence, which scared me more than the attack.

By mid-September we wondered how much longer we could hold out. When the artillery bombardment eased, snipers provided constant harassment. We found it impossible to move around the Opel factory compound and stayed crouched in the bottom of our trench under fire from grenades, mortars and tank fire.

I lost my comrade *Thur* the next day. He had told me that he had a premonition he would be killed and had expressed his deep sorrow that he would not see his mother again. I thought that he was talking nonsense, but he was right. He died instantly when a mortar shell exploded in front of our bunker.

On September 25, after being relieved, we reported to Wilson Square for a rest. Exhaustion and exposure brought on high fever, and during a lull in the fighting I made my way to the makeshift field hospital where the doctor took one look at me and sent me home. I was so weak that I needed help to get up. The pains in my stomach, head, and chest exhausted me, and I was barely conscious when Marysia visited me in the afternoon. I knew she was there; her voice was soothing.

My father was also at home with a high fever. His wounds from his escape through the sewer hadn't healed. I was weak, burning up and spitting blood. The house was filled with strangers taking refuge. Mother and my sister, Wanda, were at Baniocha. On Felinski Street, Aunt Wanda spent her time cowering in her room, terrified of the Germans, so Aunt Stacha had to cope with everything and everyone in the house. Father and I knew we couldn't stay there any longer. The attacking German Tiger tanks were a block away, and if we were caught we knew we would be shot. Sick as we were, we dressed and left the house around noon. We made our way through the communication trenches, which were under heavy tank and artillery fire. When we reached the ruins of Wilson Square, we said good-bye, not knowing if we would ever see each other again.

I went to our company's headquarters where a gruesome scene stretched out before my eyes like a waking nightmare. Bomb craters held grotesquely positioned corpses of women and children and bodies hung from the balconies of the Warsaw Cooperative Housing Colony. The once lush trees of Zoliborz had been blown out of the ground and lay entangled with casualties of the war. I finally found one of the nurses from our company, and she took me to a cellar filled with our wounded men. The enemy was very near and that evening we rejoined Reaper Company. We crawled over rubble on our hands and knees, and I noticed that I wasn't cold anymore. All of Zoliborz was on fire!

Heartbreak

Meanwhile the Red Army waited in perfidious silence in Praga, on the other side of the Vistula River. They promised every day to send help and told us to keep on fighting, but they never once made a serious attempt to cross the river. The Germans attacked with their huge Tiger tanks and Goliats, small fighting robot tanks. All communication broke down between our units, and each detachment ended up on its own. The Germans penetrated deeply into Zoliborz, toward Wilson Square and Krasinski Street.

General Bor-Komorowski notified London that our situation was desperate and that capitulation was inevitable unless large quantities of arms and ammunition were received right away. He also sent a message to Colonel *Zywiciel* for us to keep on fighting, if only for one more day. That night I joined my friends and we defended our buildings with my PIAT anti-tank gun against powerful enemy attacks. It was difficult to stay on my feet, but I managed to climb the ruins of the staircase and kept firing upon the attacking German tanks.

Two *Panzers* stopped below my window — one from the direction of the fire brigade building, the other from Wilson Square. I fired at one of them. Obviously I hit it, as the crew jumped out, their uniforms on fire. The Germans fell to the ground, screaming. At the same time, out of the corner of my eye, I saw the main gun of the other tank swinging around to aim at my window. Instinctively, I jumped out of the second-story window onto the grass below, breaking small bones in my ankle. Looking back, I saw a large hole where my window had been.

On Saturday, September 30, 1944 it became clear that it was impossible for us to hold Zoliborz any longer. Two upper floors of our building were on fire, and still we stayed at our posts, deafened by exploding shells and blinded by smoke. It was pure hell. Colonel *Zywiciel* ordered the company to withdraw in the direction of the Vistula. We were to cross at night and join the Russians.

The Commandos were always the first to attack and last to leave. That was our job. However, at noon, the order came to withdraw. Under the cover of smoke, creeping through ruined houses, we reached the remnants of our division gathered on Mickiewicz Street. The Germans, having thrown an armored tank division and robot Goliat tanks into an area the size of a postage stamp, found themselves at last in possession of almost the whole of Zoliborz.

The tanks caused extremely heavy damage. The Goliats blew the fire brigade building to smithereens, and I received orders to continue firing at the tanks with my PIAT antitank missile thrower. I was barely able to lift it, and fever had weakened me to the point where I was falling down every few yards. I had to lie on my back to pull the PIAT's uncooperative spring, but even in that state I managed to take out another tank. Finally, I could no longer pull the spring, and collapsed.

I came to in the late evening. The enemy fire had stopped. We reached a rendezvous point for our Zoliborz group, and awaited further orders. It was the place where I had spent happy times not so long ago visiting Marysia. I entered the dark, devastated Glass House lit only by burning buildings, wondering if Marysia was still alive. When I lurched back down the stairs, I met my startled comrades. One shouted at me, "What the hell are you doing wandering around these ruins? Are you completely mad?"

I sank down on the steps near my fellow soldiers. The situation looked hopeless, and we knew that we faced death. The Russians wanted the Germans to exterminate us and refused to send help.

On September 30 the news struck like lightning: Surrender. The word itself provoked a barrage of oaths from all sides. "Lies!" "Impossible!" All the companies were ordered to line up, and we did, still not believing what was happening. Lieutenant *Szeliga* stood before us and read the heartbreaking order from Colonel *Zywiciel*:

Soldiers!

I thank you, my dear comrades, for everything you have accomplished during these two months of fighting the enemy, for your efforts, pain, and courage.

I am proud that I had the honor to command such soldiers as you.

Remain such in the future and show the world what a Polish soldier is, he who will sacrifice everything for his country.

An hour ago, as ordered by the Supreme Commander of the Armed Forces, General Bor-Komorowski, I signed the surrender document of our group...

We are surrendering to the *Wehrmacht* as a regular army, and we will be treated according to the Geneva Convention.

I thank you once more for everything.

God be with you!

After that, everything seemed like a bad dream in slow motion. It was nearly midnight when we fell into formation and marched among the raging fires with even, measured steps, as if on parade, rifles on our shoulders. We had to remind the Germans what kind of soldiers they had been fighting for the last two months.

With officers at our flanks, we advanced toward Wilson Square, solidly lined with German tanks, where the enemy waited for us. We passed through a gate into the courtyard of a large apartment building and a chill of terror shook me when I saw the faces and uniforms of the hated enemy at such close range. The Germans surrounded us at once and confiscated our short arms, field glasses and so on. Then we marched in company formation to the middle of Wilson Square, illuminated by the flames of burning Zoliborz. There we threw down the rest of our large weapons.

I had nothing left to give.

Part VI

Prisoner-of-War

Packed in a Cattle Car

I drifted through the next four or five days in a haze of fever and battle fatigue. When I came down with a wracking cough, I prayed for a quick end, but apparently it wasn't my appointed time to die. I was so ill that I hardly knew what was happening.

Late in the afternoon of the fourth day of our capitulation, the Germans herded us like animals onto a cattle train. The general who had led the Lower Saxony *Panzer* division that we fought so fiercely in Zoliborz, congratulated us on our bravery and on the strong resistance we had put up. He said that he was proud that his men had had the opportunity to fight against such courageous soldiers.

On that note, we were pushed on board, sixty of us to each cattle car, and the train got underway. The journey was unbearable. We sat in darkness, and there wasn't enough room for all of us to sit down at the same time. I think we were all pretty much in shock. I was so weak from fever that I kept falling over, and my companions were kind enough to make room for me so that I could sit down with my back against the side of the wagon.

Hours later, the train came to a shuddering halt, and the side panel opened wide enough for an armed German guard to push through hardtack biscuits and 'coffee.' I tried to eat, but couldn't and barely sipped at the lukewarm liquid. The break and refreshments brought us out of our daze. I didn't join in the chatter, but I couldn't help hearing snatches of conversation. In addition to speculation about where we were going and how long we might be there, talk turned inevitably to the subject of escape. We knew that the train was heavily guarded and that anyone who tried to escape would be shot immediately.

We knew that we weren't going to a civilian camp like Auschwitz. We were headed west, probably into Germany itself, to a military camp. At that time I did not know that both military and civilian camps were places of extermination. The difference was only in the method used – starvation in military camps and gas chambers in civilian ones. The talking stopped after a bit, and we all fell into a fitful sleep. When a weak ray of daylight entered the barred opening, we woke up. I stayed where I was; others tried to stretch their cramped limbs. Some of my companions took turns watching from the window, trying to guess where we might be heading. When we passed through villages and towns, we waved our red-and-white armbands defiantly from the window.

Aside from the crowding and discomfort, the fear and hunger, we faced another humiliating aspect of our journey into captivity. We had been on that train for more than 12 hours, and, lacking a toilet or a chance to get out, we were forced to relieve ourselves in one corner. The stench became overpowering. That cattle car was a Pawiak Prison on wheels!

Granted, I hardly knew or cared what was going on around me. It's just as well that I was too dazed and sick to realize just how grim our prospects were. I was probably the youngest prisoner of war and, separated from most of my company and my family, I was very lonely. Had I been fully conscious, the situation would have been intolerable.

In the evening the train was shunted off the main tracks. Suddenly, we heard the blood-chilling wail of an air-raid siren. Later we heard bombs exploding and antiaircraft fire. We cheered because the Allies must be overhead on a bombing raid. And that meant that we had stopped in a major city, probably Berlin, deep into enemy territory in Germany. As the bombing drew nearer, we felt our helplessness and prayed we would not be hit. From the sounds of the attack, the Germans were getting hammered.

In the morning the train got underway again, and we spent another whole day in discomfort and hunger. I slumped against the wooden wall in a fevered stupor. My companions woke me up early the next morning to say that we had reached our destination, whatever it was. After days of darkness, we felt dazzled by the light when the side panel opened, even though it was a gray and drizzly day. We welcomed the fresh air, and an evergreen forest stretched as far as we could see. The sign by the track announced "Alten Grabow," which meant nothing to me.

Stalag XI-A

We marched a mile or so to an enormous wire-enclosed camp. Actually, I didn't march so much as stumble along with the help of a couple of my friends. Then we waited in the cold rain while they decided what to do with us. I learned that the barracks of this camp, Stalag XI-A at Alten Grabow, were full, and we would have to sleep in the open air. We had no bedding, no roof, but the ground felt soft and welcoming after the cattle-car floor.

That night the rain came down in torrents, and we had to dig channels around ourselves in order not to drown. The next morning I couldn't get up, and that meant I couldn't eat, because you only got food if you stood in line. I had reached the point of not caring. I lay on the soaked ground, wishing all this would end. My friends smuggled food to me whenever they could, even though they risked being

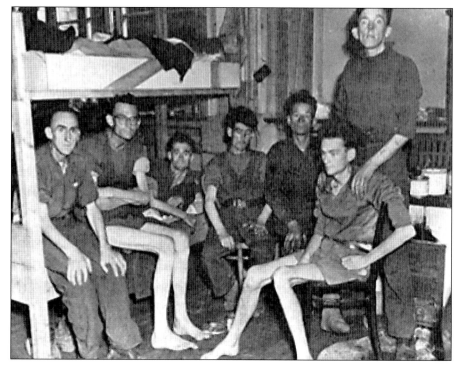

Hospital.

shot if they'd been caught.

The camp held hundreds of thousands of men, but the Germans kept detailed records of each prisoner. Soon I received my prisoner-of-war number, 45517.

Finally, a British prisoner serving as a camp medic looked me over. He gave me the good news that he had assigned me, with several friends who were also ill, to the camp hospital. The bad news, he added, was that the hospital was three miles away and I would have to get there on my own two feet.

I lurched along like an old drunk and fell down a lot. Each time I fell, I was convinced that I wouldn't get up again. But I did, and somehow we made it to the Gross Lubars Lazarett, which was a pathetic excuse for a medical facility!

The "hospital" was a flimsy affair, wooden barracks with board beds. The Polish section for T.B. (tuberculosis) patients was filled, and eventually they found room for us in one of the Italian barracks for the terminally ill. The room was filthy, the beds infested with bugs from the dirty straw mattresses, but it was better than the wet ground. We even had one blanket each.

I burned up one minute, shivered the next, and I coughed up blood. Many of the other men in the ward were in the same dismal shape. There were no nurses, but in the morning a doctor arrived and examined each one of us. His considered opinion was that I was dying, but his cynical prescription was "plenty of rest and good food!"

In the weeks that followed, the days passed very slowly, and there was barely enough food to keep us alive. At seven a.m. we got half a quart of bitter liquid, neither coffee nor tea. At noon we got a cup of turnip soup without any salt, fat or potatoes. Our evening meal consisted of a piece of black bread and a spoonful of red beet jam.

Time dragged by, and I lay in bed, weaker than ever, convinced that I would not leave there alive. The grimness of camp life surpassed anything that I had known so far, and I slipped into a deep depression of hopelessness. The uprising had instilled in the freedom fighters a purpose that transcended dangers and risks. Prepared to fight to the end, we had been ordered to surrender instead. Sometimes I wondered whether it would not have been vastly preferable to go down fighting.

Although I was only 15, I felt as if I had already lived several lifetimes. Now, weakened by fever, that wracking tubercular cough, starvation, and exhaustion— mental and physical — I felt very old. But I had been fortunate to grow up with good nutrition and a healthy environment. That underlying strength and my youth worked in my favor to keep me alive in that hellhole of a camp.

The days passed in a monotonous blur, and boredom posed a major problem for us. We all risked losing our minds and did what we could to avoid the mental demons that prey on prisoners of war. Many nationalities were represented, and each one reacted differently to camp life. Those from the most affluent countries were least able to stand the suffering. The Germans treated the Russian prisoners by far the worst. The "hospital" was supposed to be in quarantine, but we visited each other to break the boredom and monotony.

The British played a lot of football, what Americans call soccer, and they tended to be friendly, shy, and reserved. They were thin to begin with, but they looked like walking skeletons after a few weeks of prison-camp food. But then, we all did.

We communicated with pidgin bits of language, signs, and little sketches. The Sikhs and Ghurkas, British Army soldiers from the colony of India, tried to teach me whist, a card game similar to bridge, and I attempted to teach them Polish.

The Dutch were on friendly terms with everyone, but like the rest of the prisoners they ignored the French, who talked their way out of forced labor by openly going along with the Germans.

From time to time, the sound of Allied bombers overhead inspired every man to cheer until his lungs were ready to burst, but we also dealt with the ever-present fear that they might drop bombs on our stalag. A camp rumor had it that our barracks were located over a munitions factory, which only fueled our fears of ending up on the receiving end of an Allied bombing raid.

Along about November something happened that helped to boost my flagging spirits and maybe saved my life. Danuta and Barbara, identical twins who had been nurses during our battle in Zoliborz, turned up in Stalag XI-A. They found me and began visiting when they could. They smuggled food to me even though it would have meant their lives had they been caught. Daily, they made repeated trips through the food line, but because they looked so much alike the Germans were confused and didn't notice the extra trips. The food was mostly pea soup, but every bit helped stave off starvation. They even had news of my girl friend, Marysia: She had escaped with her mother.

A short time before Christmas, Danuta and Barbara and all the other girls in the camp were herded together to be shipped off to a women's camp somewhere. They must have resisted, for many were beaten viciously by the German guards and left seriously injured on stretchers in the snow for hours until the train arrived. We were all devastated by the loss of the girls, who had done so much to brighten our lives. In fact, their departure made a lot of the hardened veterans realize just what the girls had meant to all of us, and I saw a number of them weep openly for these brave young women who had suffered such harsh treatment.

Christmas was beyond dismal. Alone, bereft, without the friendly ministrations of Danuta and Barbara, homesick for my family, I also had to deal with the loss of friends I had made in the stalag. Many mornings I would wake up next to a corpse. A lot of wounded prisoners continued to arrive at the hospital, but most of them hadn't been injured in battle. They were hurt doing forced labor in nearby mines and stone quarries. One fellow befriended me. He was a lively Scot who carried dogeared photos of his family. Using a mixture of German and English, he told me that prisoners from the main camp had to work 12 hours a day, seven days a week, on starvation-level rations. They came to the so-called hospital because they were injured working or beaten by the guards for not working fast enough. My Scottish friend came because he had been beaten so badly that he had lost his mind. Two days later he died from those injuries. When I found out, I was horribly depressed.

I also knew that forced labor would mean my demise.

It became a matter of steeling myself to do whatever it took to survive. The arrival of the new year changed nothing, and incoming prisoners reported that the Red Army occupied Poland and that the Allies were getting closer to our stalag. Fortunately, as there were so many prisoners, it was easy enough to use my ill health as an excuse to stay in the "hospital." Main camp conditions were just as bad, if not worse than the POW "hospitals": constant damp, cold, crowding and vermin, without washing or laundry facilities. On top of everything else, my gums had receded and my teeth were so loose, I was afraid they would fall out any minute.

Liberation

On March 3, 1945 I turned 16, and the distant but constant, rumbling noise of advancing American artillery was my birthday present. Liberation started to look like a real possibility when we heard that the Americans had reached the Elbe River. Waiting was more demoralizing than ever, because we still had no idea when we would be liberated or if we would still be alive. We waited in anxious anticipation, and we strained at our confines, yearning to be free.

Liberation.

The 3rd of May, the Polish National holiday, became even more special for me. That morning, thousands of American Army trucks arrived at Stalag XI-A to collect American, British, Belgian, French and Dutch prisoners of war. All other nationalities had to wait for the Red Army to arrive. I didn't want to wait; I wanted to go right then and there. I stared at the trucks, wishing with all my heart for a chance to leave. I knew that I was one of the thousands of prisoners just as desperate to exit that evil place.

When the opportunity presented itself, I could not pass it up. Prisoners crowded around the gates, watching with longing as the Army trucks filled up with Americans and British. The *Wehrmacht* guarded the gates, but in that crowd suddenly I saw a chance to duck out under the arms of a guard trying to contain the rest of the POWs. I mingled with the soldiers being liberated and for two hours I watched them fill up the trucks. I was so starved for freedom, I decided to risk leaving my buddies behind. I spotted an American I had made friends with sitting in a truck. He noticed me and signaled to me to jump on. In a few seconds, helped along by the strong hands of the Yanks, I was on my way – free of Stalag XI-A and the bondage of Germany's Third Reich.

I was free at last.

Epilogue

War is an unimaginable horror, but it is also full of heroic deeds. I have tried to erase the nightmares and evil memories and to draw inspiration from the great sacrifices I witnessed, acts of love seldom encountered during peace-time. Over time, my wartime experiences strengthened my resolve to appreciate the beauty and value of life, and I became determined to pursue a creative — not destructive — life and career. I carried the inspiring legacy of the white eagle to America, where I enjoyed unique opportunities and became a successful architect. Nowhere else in the world would I have been able to develop my full potential.

There was only one 1944 Warsaw Uprising and yet it encompassed multitudes of events that changed history: brutal suppression by the Germans, total destruction of a beautiful and historic city, the murder of 250,000 civilians in two short months, the devious and evil hypocrisy of Stalin, the ominous silence of Roosevelt and Churchill, the lack of adequate Allied support, the hopeless attempt to prevent Soviet occupation of Poland, and the deadly struggle of young boys and girls against the evils of fascism and communism.

The Warsaw Uprising compounded Poland's long legacy as a defender of freedom and left an indelible mark on national character, but it also became the subject of bitter criticism and conjecture. Some have viewed the uprising as an unmitigated political and military disaster, saying that it resulted in the destruction of the capital and of the Underground army, which was desperately needed to fight the Soviet Union's evil empire. But the boys and girls who laid down their lives for freedom in the uprising were neither politicians nor military strategists. We were just fighting bravely against the vicious, methodical extermination of all Poles simply because they were Poles. Like our Jewish brothers and sisters in the 1943 Warsaw Ghetto Uprising, the Christian youth chose to die fighting. With homemade grenades, youngsters attacked the Germans' well-equipped, sophisticated army and fought squadrons of bombers, heavy artillery and Hitler's crack armored regiments. We young Poles believed with all our hearts and souls that ours was a righteous cause worth dying for.

I believe that history has proved the young people were right beyond a shadow of a doubt, and the skeptical critics were wrong. The Solidarity movement of the 1980s, which contributed to the downfall of the Soviet empire, was the brave extension of the Polish resolve to be free. Solidarity leaders freely admit that they were carrying out the legacy of the Polish Legions in World War I and the Warsaw Uprising in World War II. The example of a generation willing to make the supreme sacrifice in defense of freedom and democracy provided a vivid template for the Solidarity movement.

I am infinitely grateful that in my lifetime I was allowed to see the restoration of the white eagle proudly wearing the crown of freedom, bestowing its legacy upon independent, free and democratic Poland. I am gratified and moved that my comrades in arms can now rest in the peace they deserve in the military cemetery in Warsaw — rest in peace knowing that their deaths were not in vain, assured that their defense of independence will never be forgotten by all freedom-loving people.

Glossary

Allies: Members of an alliance, friendly nations. In World War II, the Allies were Great Britain, the U.S., the Soviet Union (USSR), Poland and other countries united against the Axis powers—Germany, Italy, and Japan.

blitzkrieg: A sudden, fast military offensive usually by land and air forces combined, from the German words blitz (lightning) and krieg (war).

capitulation: Making concessions, agreeing to give something to an enemy after negotiating specific terms. Contrast with "surrender"—to give up completely.

Communism: A system of government in which one political party plans and controls the economy without opposition, claiming to make progress toward having all goods equally shared by the people.

Communist: A political party dedicated to the overthrow of capitalism and democracy. In World War II, the Communist Party that ruled the Soviet Union supported the Polish Communist Party, which took over Poland after the defeat of Germany.

D-Day: A day when a military operation is due to begin, most famously the day on which the Allied forces invaded France during World War II (June 6, 1944).

DDT: DichloroDiphenylTrichloroethane, an insecticide used to kill disease-carrying insects in World War II prison camps. DDT is so poisonous that it has been banned in the U.S. for most uses since 1972.

Geneva Convention: An international agreement establishing rules for the treatment of prisoners of war. The first agreements were formulated at a convention in 1864 in Geneva, Switzerland.

Gestapo: The secret security police in Nazi Germany, known for its terrorist methods.

ghetto: Formerly, the restricted quarter of many European cities in which Jews were required to live. During World War II, the Germans confined Jews in the Warsaw Ghetto.

government-in-exile: A temporary government formed in a foreign land by exiles who hope to rule when their country is liberated. Polish leaders fled to England to form a government-in-exile during World War II.

incendiary: a bomb or ammunition containing chemicals that produce intensely hot fire when exploded.

Luftwaffe: The German air force before and during World War II, from the German words luft (air) and waffe (weapon).

Panzer: A German armored vehicle or tank, especially the type used during World War II, from a German word for armor.

POW: A prisoner of war.

pseudonym: A false name, in wartime a code name taken to keep a person's true name secret.

puppet: A government or an army controlled by a foreign country that may impose hardships on those governed.

quinsy: A painful, pus-filled infection of the tonsils, usually with fever.

Soviet Union: From 1922 through 1991, a communist country that included Russia and 14 smaller countries; also called the USSR, or Union of Soviet Socialist Republics.

SS: German abbreviation for Schutzstaffel (defense staff), an elite unit of the Nazi party that initially served as Hitler's personal guard. Its combat arm, the Waffen SS, grew into a force of over 950,000 men with a reputation for committing atrocities in occupied territories. Many of its leaders were condemned by the Nuremberg Trials after World War II and executed as war criminals.

stalag: a German camp for prisoners of war.

Sten gun: A lightweight submachine gun named for its English inventors.

storm troops: Nazi militia created by Hitler in 1921 that helped him to power but became less important to him than the SS.

treason: betrayal of one's country by waging war against it or by consciously and purposely acting to aid its enemies.

trusty: A convict or prisoner regarded as worthy of trust and therefore granted special privileges.

TB: Tuberculosis, an infectious disease of the lungs characterized by the coughing up of mucus and sputum, fever, weight loss, and chest pain.

typhus: Infectious disease caused by Rickettsia bacteria, usually transmitted by fleas, lice, or mites, and characterized by severe headache, high fever, depression, delirium, and red rashes on the skin. Also called "camp fever" or "prison fever."

ubermensch: German for "elite man," a superman or person with great powers and abilities, used by Nazi officials to describe themselves as superior to other people.

underground: A hidden or concealed organization fostering or planning hostile activities or the overthrow of a government in power, such as an occupying military government.

uprising: A revolt by the people, a rebellion against a government or its policies.

National History Day

Each year, more than 500,000 students choose historical topics related to the annual National History Day (NHD) theme. Beginning in the fall, students in grades 6-12 conduct extensive primary and secondary research through libraries, archives, museums, oral history interviews, and historic sites. After analyzing and interpreting their sources and drawing conclusions about their topics' significance in history, students then present their work in original papers, exhibits, performances, or documentaries. These products are entered into competitions in the spring at local, state, and national levels where they are evaluated by professional historians and educators. The program culminates with the national competition each June held at the University of Maryland at College Park. For more information see National History Day's website at www.nhd.org.

National History Day, Inc.(NHD) is an educational organization that is transforming the way history is taught and learned. NHD helps teachers meet educational standards; disseminates high quality curriculum materials; and sponsors challenging contests that teach students the critical skills they need to be effective citizens in the 21st century. The combination of creativity and scholarship built into the organization's programs anticipated current educational reforms, making NHD a leading model of performance-based learning.

Acknowledgments

During the years of writing this book and producing the video I was assisted by many individuals who unwaveringly believed that the Legacy of the White Eagle would inspire young people and excite enthusiasm for the study of history. I am most deeply indebted to Kimball Hart, fellow Yaleman, and a long-time friend of mine and of Poland. When the trauma of my youthful war experiences overcame me, he quietly prodded me and insisted that I continue to make the story of this epic struggle known to younger generations. He is responsible for bringing the book and the DVD to life with his tireless and skillful management of all aspects of the project—a true labor of love.

I was fortunate that during the project's culminating years I had great support from the Polish Embassy and Ambassador Przemyslaw Grudzinski. The enthusiasm of Boleslaw Winid, patriot, fellow Varsovian, and a Chargé d'Affaires at the Polish Embassy, never flagged. His steadfast support for educating American students about the Warsaw Uprising of 1944 was crucial to the completion of this project.

It was especially important that many veterans of the Polish Underground Army were able to contribute directly to the story through personal interviews: a painful process given the subject. Included in that group are: the author's comrades in arms from the 9th Commando Company, Wieslaw Alfred Kaczmarek, Janusz Prazmo, and Gustaw Budzynski, the Deputy Commander; frontline nurses Maria Krzywicka Rukszan, Danuta Kolodziejska Pollard, and her twin sister Barbara Kolodziejska; and Maria Chojecka "Kama" of the distinguished Anti-Gestapo Commando Unit. These survivors provided personal insight that greatly enriched this chronicle of the Warsaw odyssey.

The distinguished historian, Professor Wojciech Roszkowski, provided the historical background of the heroic uprising against brutal Nazi oppressors.

A picture is worth a thousand words. Without the professional skill and enthusiasm of the documentary film producer, Gary Rowe, the story would have remained only on the pages of the book. His on-the-scene filming at Auschwitz, Pawiak Prison, and the Szucha Avenue torture chambers brought the story to life and into the twenty-first century.

While in Warsaw the outstanding Polish documentary film producer, Krzysztof Wojciechowski, volunteered many hours of free filmmaking because he believed that the story of Warsaw should not be forgotten. He deserves my thanks and appreciation.

The Museum of the Warsaw Uprising in Warsaw provided immeasurable assistance by opening its rich photo, video, and audio archives for use in the DVD. Director Jan Oldakowski and the staff went beyond the call of duty to assure that the story of the 1944 Uprising would be shown in American schools. We gratefully acknowledge this very generous gift.

Since many of the individuals were interviewed in Polish, extensive translation was necessary. Jan Jurek, a patriotic Polish student at Boston College, spent many days translating and deserves recognition and appreciation.

I am very grateful to my editor, Monica Bradsher, for her endless patience and for her skillful ability to bring out the essence of the story. She is the best of the best. I also want to thank Cathy Gorn, Executive Director of National History Day, for her unfailing support and for making history exciting and absorbing. I owe much to Mary Speer, who struggled valiantly with Polish spelling and for her tireless and patient work in transcribing the manuscript. Last but not least, I record my gratitude to my wife, Catharine, who endured uncomplainingly the years of my absorption with the project and assisted in many ways.

The Central Archives of Modern Records in Poland generously gave permission to use in the DVD their archival film footage and photographs of the Warsaw Uprising. We are extremely grateful to Director Jolanta Louchin. These documentary films form a very important part of our educational project.